Effective Communication at Work

Vicki McLeod

Effective Communication at Work

Speaking and Writing Well in the Modern Workplace

ROCKRIDGE PRESS

For general information on our other products and services or to obtain technical support, please contact our Customer Care Department within the United States at (866) 744-2665, or outside the United States at (510) 253-0500.

Rockridge Press publishes its books in a variety of electronic and print formats. Some content that appears in print may not be available in electronic books, and vice versa.

TRADEMARKS: Rockridge Press and the Rockridge Press logo are trademarks or registered trademarks of Callisto Media Inc. and/or its affiliates, in the United States and other countries, and may not be used without written permission. All other trademarks are the property of their respective owners. Rockridge Press is not associated with any product or vendor mentioned in this book.

Interior and Cover Designer: Regina Stadnik
Art Producer: Tom Hood
Editor: Anne Lowrey
Production Editor: Matthew Burnett
Author photograph courtesy © Wendy D Photo

ISBN: Print 978-1-64611-591-4 | Ebook 978-1-64611-592-1

R0

To Thomas Ian McLeod, a most patient communicator, who in every way exemplifies the spirit of loving partnership

CONTENTS

PART 1
Speak and Write Better at Work   1

PART 2
Better Work Relationships 75

INTRODUCTION

I n 1994, I launched my strategic communications consultancy Main Street Communications Ltd. We worked with businesses and government agencies, supporting their external and internal communications. In those days, very few civic governments had a formal communications function. The Internet was new, and clients were cautious about venturing into an unknown space. In addition to crafting comprehensive communications plans for them, we worked hard to convince clients to consider using the World Wide Web as a tool to connect with their stakeholders and customers.

Nearly 20 years later, I found myself making the same arguments to clients—this time about establishing social media profiles. I've now worked with hundreds of businesses, organizations, and individuals to help them overcome their reluctance to engage in social networking with clients and customers. The introduction of new communication strategies and technologies brought significant change. For some, this was positive. For others, it was a struggle.

I have always had a strong commitment to personal development work, believing that human potential is one of the last great unexplored frontiers. In both my corporate practice and my private coaching practice, I have had the privilege to work directly with professionals at all levels. For nearly 30 years I have closely observed the habits, behaviors, and traits that make good leaders great and stood shoulder to shoulder with them as they solved problems, navigated conflict, and addressed personal and professional challenges. I have seen firsthand the positive impact of effective communication, not only on the lives and careers of the professionals with whom I've worked but also on the success of their workplace projects, initiatives, and strategies.

I lived more than half my life in a wholly analog environment and understand the mental shift required to embrace the technology of the digital age. The demands of the digital world and its never-ending learning curve can be exhausting. Helping clients cross the digital divide made me realize that they require additional skills to be successful—especially in managing the scope, scale, and pace of digital engagement. The ability to manage time, prioritize, avoid distraction, and focus on what truly mattered to them and their businesses became paramount. In 2015, I wrote a tiny book called *#UNTRENDING, A Field Guide to Social Media That Matters. How to Post, Tweet, and Like Your Way to a More Meaningful Life* (First Choice, 2016). I wrote it as a guide to using social media in a meaningful way. It aimed to help the reader use platforms like Facebook, Twitter, and Instagram to communicate with authenticity and meaning. I proposed that in order to craft meaningful posts, we actually need to get offline—to disconnect in order to reconnect. I urged readers to find more time for offline pursuits, to dive deeply into life's offerings and fully digest them, and to then come back to technology enriched and fulfilled.

I've devoted more than a decade to researching and writing about the intersection of the analog and digital worlds. Social media, e-mail, chat platforms, instant messaging, and texting have dramatically impacted the way we communicate at home and at work, but we must be mindful of the need to connect offline and to be fully present at home and on the job. In this book, I draw extensively on my professional and personal experience as a consultant and as a professional coach. I hope that this book will educate, inform, and inspire you to take on the challenges posed by communicating effectively as we navigate the future together. I further hope it provides you the necessary insight and the confidence to speak up, show up, and contribute fully in your life and work.

PART 1

Speak and Write Better at Work

CHAPTER 1

WHY COMMUNICATING WELL AT WORK IS IMPORTANT

C ommunication is a fascinating area to study. It is the way that people engage and interact and our primary means of human connection. Beyond its transactional purpose—sending and receiving messages—it involves a subtle interplay of empathy, intuition, intention, and comprehension. Done well, it deepens relationships, builds trust, and is a tool for complex and nuanced problem-solving. It helps us avoid misunderstandings and conflict and resolve them when they arise. Effective communication is at the heart of successful, happy relationships and healthy workplaces. We want people to see and hear us. We desire real understanding and long to connect. Nowhere is this more evident than in the rapid worldwide adaptation of digital communications technology.

The digital age is revolutionizing how we communicate. Since you are reading this book, you are aware that today's working world demands that individuals possess top-notch communication skills. Think about how vital it is to exchange ideas in important meetings or to convey the right information to new hires. What about offering supportive feedback to colleagues or asking your boss for a raise or new opportunity? We spend most of our days engaged in our work. The social bonds we make with colleagues in the workplace often last a lifetime.

Almost everybody has different communication styles. There are generational and cultural differences in every office. This is especially true now that we are living and working in more global environments. Expectations around technology and the aptitude required to use it effectively may vary widely. Older generations of workers are eager to pass on their expertise and mentor younger generations, but they may be clumsy when it comes to adopting new technologies. Today's young workers seek a well-rounded life, expect to enjoy their work, and want opportunities to use and introduce new ideas and skill sets. They comfortably use technology to support and enhance their lifestyles. Workers of all ages and stages of their career want to feel valued and acknowledged.

Given these considerations, it is no wonder that communication is one of the top skills that employers look for in new hires. Employers consider communication a "soft skill." These are desirable qualities that do not depend on acquired knowledge; rather, they include common sense, the ability to deal with people, and a positive flexible attitude. While hard skills are generally taught—database management, for example, or how to pilot a plane—soft skills are personality traits that have to do with attitude and inclination. These are transferable skills that one can apply in a variety of situations. Professionals who have a good grasp of the "soft" skills can easily learn or be trained in the "hard" or technical skills required for roles across and upward in the organization or business.

See for yourself: Do a quick Internet search of the most desirable workplace skills. You will find communication skills on every list. Communication skills are not just important when you are interviewing for a new position or looking for professional advancement. They are equally essential if you are in a position of leadership in an organization or running your own business.

Take Jason, for example. Jason is a hardworking entrepreneur who runs a stable and successful home renovation business. He has four employees, and his biggest challenges are motivating his crew and setting and enforcing clear expectations around quality. Jason admits that communication is his primary problem. He does not like conflict and is not fully comfortable in his role as crew boss. Jason is in good company.

According to a 2016 *Harvard Business Review* report, 69% of managers are uncomfortable communicating with their employees. Jason finds his work and the job site stressful and anxiety-inducing. He dreams of moving from home renovation into home building, where he will work with subcontractors and other professionals who will be dealing with their own crews on his behalf, but this will not solve the problem. He will still need to use critical communication skills, conflict management, problem-solving tools, and negotiating skills to develop the necessary relationships for his business to expand. Either way, he must deal with his own lack of skill in the crucial area of interpersonal communication if he is to succeed at any level.

Think about this regarding your own workplace. If you are a team leader or manager, you may be like Jason, needing to direct the work of others and shouldering the responsibility for the team's success. You may have a manager like Jason, one of the many who are too uncomfortable or too poorly equipped to communicate effectively with their teams. Jason doesn't lack desire, but he lacks skill. He and others like him are very proficient at their required tasks—Jason is an excellent builder—but communication skills just don't come naturally to him. People like Jason need to learn, practice, and develop in the soft skills areas to grow to the next level in their careers. The good news is that people can learn these skills, and with practice we can all become stronger communicators.

The Power of Effective Communication

What is effective communication? At its most basic, communication is how we send and receive messages. Whether we are communicating verbally, nonverbally, or in written form, we are first attempting to clearly articulate and convey thoughts, feelings, and ideas. Our goal is to get our message across.

The second part of the communications equation is receiving the message. This involves engaged or active listening, reading cues, or observing and confirming what we have heard. To determine whether the sending and receiving of messages has been effective, it is important to understand the goal of the communication itself. Perhaps you are imparting important information to a colleague about a specific work process or safety concern. You may be looking to develop team spirit or build company morale by soliciting ideas and engagement from your team. Your goal might simply be to build relationships and trust to deepen human connection in the workplace. If you step back to identify the purpose and meaning of the communication, for both the sender and receiver, you can then assess its effectiveness.

Thus, effective communication is not just about sending clear messages and confirming that they are received—it is about validating mutual understanding. It involves more than just speaking, listening, writing, and reading. To communicate effectively, we need to use all our senses to express, interpret, and comprehend meaning.

Workplace Benefits of Better Communication

In the opening to this chapter, we talked about why effective communication is important. Let's explore further.

Clear, straightforward communication fosters good working relationships and results in good staff morale and higher productivity. Happy workplaces can attract and retain the talent they need to be effective and profitable. Business processes and systems, from human resources policies to building company infrastructure, rely on comprehensive, accurate, and timely information in order to flow smoothly. At every stage of the development and design of such systems, people are required to communicate well. In the digital age, with multiple communication touch points, this has become more challenging than ever.

To be competitive in today's marketplace, businesses must embrace innovation and find ways to move and adapt into new and expanding markets. In fast-moving business environments, breakdowns in communication are costly. Poor communication can drive wedges between teams, negatively impact customer service and sales, and poison the corporate culture, resulting in lost productivity and high staff turnover. Successful companies rely on the consistent expertise and interpersonal skills of their staff to collaborate on projects of all kinds—generating, analyzing, assessing, and prioritizing new ideas and initiatives. A high-performing workforce is essential to a company's success.

We've established that employers prize good communication skills. Interestingly, it works both ways—employees value effective communication from their employers as well. According to a 2019 report issued by the global recruiting and staffing agency Aerotek, clear, transparent communication makes the list of the *Top Ten Most Important Benefits* ranked by employees.

Perhaps you have worked in an organization where you were undervalued or where employees were shielded from the company's goals and expectations. Such an environment can be stressful, or, worse, it can become hostile or toxic. It is difficult to stay motivated and engaged if your management team does not value your opinion and you have no sense of how your work connects to the bigger picture. It is natural to want management to take your ideas seriously and recognize you for your work. It is also important to give and receive timely and useful feedback about performance and to have a clear understanding of how you contribute to the company's success. All of these rely on developing effective channels of communication, both online and off.

WHAT DOES GOOD COMMUNICATION LOOK LIKE?

Good communicators are attentive to detail. They understand that words matter and that we convey meaning not only through word choice but also through the time, place, and medium by which we deliver those words. They are alert to communication cues and signals such as body language, facial expressions, tone of voice, eye contact, and gesture. They understand and respect diverse communication styles, cultures, experiences, and generational differences. They are engaged listeners and ask questions to clarify meaning and explore ideas more deeply. Good communicators understand that it is important to build trust and be empathetic. They are patient and positive.

In both speaking and writing, they are clear, concise and to the point. Their communication is friendly and professional, respecting their coworkers' time and often limited availability. They are responsive to requests and avoid making assumptions, passing judgment, or getting personal in the event of misunderstandings or conflict. They are on time and prepared for meetings, whether online or offline. They have a high level of self-awareness and work to find common ground.

Becoming a good communicator takes practice. Here are some examples of good and bad communication in the workplace. See if you can identify the qualities that contribute to either effective or ineffective communication.

- Kate is open and friendly. She begins most conversations with a smile and makes eye contact before she begins speaking. She pauses frequently to allow her coworkers to contribute and asks questions to encourage them to engage.

- Greta receives dozens of e-mail requests for information daily. She replies to them the same day, and if she doesn't have the required information, she provides a time frame for when coworkers can expect a response.

- Michelle prefers to communicate face-to-face. When she stops by her coworkers' desks, she checks to see how busy they are and asks if they have time to discuss the task. If not, she sets up a time to meet or covers her question in an e-mail.

- Jon becomes easily overwhelmed by too much verbal information. He routinely sends follow-up e-mails summarizing and confirming his understanding of action items and information from meetings.

- Devin typically answers requests with one-word responses, terse to the point of rudeness. These require several follow-ups to elicit needed information.

- Nala is a bright, driven extrovert. In meetings, she takes over the agenda and dominates the discussion with her ideas.

- Emily checks her smartphone continually throughout meetings, texting under the table to coworkers in other parts of the building. She makes little eye contact and frequently asks to have the conversation repeated.

- Abe avoids using technology to interact and resists training on new tools. He requests multiple meetings to accomplish tasks and often lacks critical information distributed via digital platforms.

These people all have different communication styles, preferences, and life experiences. They all do some things very well and have areas where they can improve. If you recognize a little of yourself in any of these examples, let me reassure you—you are in good company. They represent real-world clients who learned to play to their communications strengths and mitigate their weaknesses through commitment and practice.

ADAPTING YOUR PERSONAL COMMUNICATION STYLE

We all have a personal style when it comes to communication. Our natural inclination toward being introverted and soft-spoken or extroverted and more assertive and even our culture or upbringing influence the way we engage and interact with others. To be successful in the workplace (and outside it), it is important to understand your personal style of communication and to be willing to adapt if necessary.

There are various formal assessments that you can use to identify personality types and their related communication styles. Some of these include Myers-Briggs, DISC, Straight Talk, and the Enneagram Personality Test. Many offer excellent and useful insight. For our purposes, let's keep the discussion of styles general. There is an assessment you can take on page 137 to help you identify your own communication strengths and challenges.

Beyond the traditional segmentation of communication styles into passive, aggressive, passive-aggressive, and assertive, people generally tend to fall somewhere on the introversion and extroversion scale in terms of how they communicate and which communication channels they prefer. People also differ in how they process and comprehend information. Some of us are analytical and need data, hard facts, and details. This group prefers precise language and clarity. People who are more intuitive tend to focus on the big picture and trust their instincts.

Introverts are often good listeners who need more time to consider and process ideas. The same goes for "thinkers" who appreciate facts, are deliberate in their communications, and tend toward caution. Extroverts tend to be linear thinkers who process quickly and out loud, often needing to talk through scenarios to solve problems. Some people are quite expressive and others more restrained. Many people value harmony above all else and are apt to be peacemakers who attune easily to others' feelings. Others like to compete and engage in robust debate, seeing themselves as take-charge people who value quick decisions and action. People also have different functional strengths such as written skills, oral skills, and reading or listening skills.

Most of us have some blend of styles that serve us differently in different circumstances. What is important is that you develop an awareness of your own styles and preferences and take steps to identify and understand the styles and preferences of others. This is particularly useful because there are bound to be times you need to adapt your own style to communicate successfully.

We also need to discern which channels are most appropriate for different types of communication. If you are a shy introvert, you may prefer the asynchronous nature of e-mail and texting to communicate. However, e-mailing and texting may not be appropriate when a face-to-face conversational exchange is needed. Outgoing extroverts may prefer to talk everything through and come to rapid-fire decisions, but company policies and procedures may dictate that you summarize projects in writing or that you provide bullet-point overviews to team members prior to discussion and decision. A healthy workplace appreciates, respects, and values different communication styles.

The Perks and Challenges of Communication in the Digital Age

We live in a time when our ability to communicate with each other is unparalleled. With the Internet, we are less restricted by time or geography than ever before and can connect with one another across the globe with unprecedented ease. These advances are transforming how we communicate.

Let's examine a typical contemporary workplace. Nearly every workstation will have an individual PC or laptop. Employees will have a personal smartphone and perhaps a company smartphone or tablet as well. In addition to your workstation, you may also have a laptop that you bring back and forth to work or use when you travel. Because of wireless technology and cloud storage, we can access and share our work files from any location. Tools and platforms such as Dropbox, Basecamp, Slack, and Google Drive enable project teams to work together in real time from anywhere, across the world and across cultures. Videoconferencing via Skype, Zoom, GoToMeeting, and other platforms means we can enjoy face-to-face communication away from the office. Add to the mix e-mail, text messaging, voice memos, FaceTime . . . we need not only to be effective communicators in terms of exchanging ideas, we also need to be skilled at using a wide variety of technologies and understand the norms and etiquettes of their use.

With the advent of social media, I began training business and community leaders in how to use it effectively. I asked them to imagine that they were visitors to a new planet—a planet called "Social Media." Taking the travel analogy further, each of the social media platforms—Twitter, Facebook, LinkedIn, Instagram—is like a different country on the planet with its own set of customs, norms, and etiquettes, just as countries have here on Earth. As good travelers, it is important to understand and respect these customs.

If we apply this analogy to today's workplace, we are all required to travel to the planet "Effective Communication" and navigate a multitude of communication channels and their various etiquettes. While digital communication has provided us with an amazing array of tools and opportunities to communicate, it has also introduced new norms that have made the process of sending, receiving, and understanding ideas much more complicated. The good news is we can learn to navigate the complexities wisely and well.

HOW HAS DIGITAL COMMUNICATION CHANGED US?

One of the great benefits of digital communication is the speed by which we can convey information and accomplish tasks. We can make deals instantaneously via e-mail, using digital signatures to sign off. On-demand, "just-in-time" information is at our fingertips. The pace, scope, and scale of information is constantly accelerating. However, the immediacy of information creates a sense of urgency that results in shorter attention spans and expectations of faster response times.

There is a commonly cited statistic that the average human attention span is now at about eight seconds, equivalent to that of a goldfish. According to the inbound marketing software company HubSpot, typical office workers check their e-mail 30 times per hour and the average person picks up his or her phone more than 1,500 times per week. This consumes an astonishing three hours and 16 minutes a day! Good communication skills become even more important in the digital age when getting someone's attention, and keeping it, is a genuine challenge.

Multiple communication channels mean there are more places to keep track of and check throughout the working day. If you are in a consumer-facing industry or a customer service role, you may use multiple channels just to stay connected with customers. Add to that channels for internal communication—e-mail, company chats, intranet feeds, webinars, and other online training sessions and teleconferences. There is also a world of technology beyond screens and keyboards. The Internet of Things (IoT) and the smart technology it uses are already in common use at home. If it hasn't already, this technology will soon find its way to a workplace near you. Each of these channels brings its own specific technical requirements, etiquettes, and norms.

Marshal McLuhan, an internationally renowned media theorist who essentially predicted the Internet back in the 1960s, said famously that "the medium is the message," referring to the way that the tools we use to communicate shape the communication itself. The digital age has made some forms of communication nearly obsolete while introducing new forms, forcing us to adapt to be effective. Consider what a rare thing it is now to receive a long-form written letter via regular post—what we now call "snail mail." Even lengthy e-mails and text posts are outdated. In contemporary communications, clarity and brevity are key. Communication in the digital age is shorter, faster, and higher volume.

ARE WE COMMUNICATING BETTER OR WORSE NOW?

There are many opinions on the positive or negative effects of increased digital communication and its impact. We are the first generation that has had to deal with the integration of analog and digital tools in the workplace, and we are often learning as we go. Whether you feel we are communicating better or worse now may well depend on your generation.

In one of my previous books, *Digital Legacy Plan, A Guide to the Personal and Practical Elements of Your Digital Life Before You Die* (Self-Counsel Press, 2019) coauthored by Angela Crocker, we explored the various generations and how they approach the digital age. As noted in that book, the dates and names of each cohort vary depending on the source and are not definitive.

The current generation, known as Gen Z or Centennials, is the first one to live in the digital age from birth. They have never known a world without the Internet and have always had access to computers and handheld devices. Having hugely diverse digital skills, Centennials grew up in the world of multiple communications channels, where instant messaging and emoji-speak are familiar and often preferred.

For a baby boomer, someone born between 1945 and 1964, who lived the shift from manual typewriters to electronic keyboards, the distractions and interruptions inherent in digital communication may be difficult to navigate. This is especially difficult for those born before 1945. People from these generations may well embrace the digital life, but many prefer picking up the phone or dropping by in person to communicate.

Generation X, born between 1965 and 1976, and Millennials or Gen Y (born between 1977 and 1995) are transitional generations. We often credit Gen X with inventing the Internet, Wi-Fi, online communities, social media, and more. Millennials have never known a world without electronic calculators, Internet research, or video games. These generations embrace social media and have pioneered more flexible work-life arrangements, including the use of technology to work remotely.

Each generation has learned to cope with emerging technology and adapt to the subsequent cultural and social shifts that these advances require. In today's workplace, you can find up to five generations working together. This creates the potential for intergenerational conflict, particularly when it comes to engaging with new communications technology. Add to this the global nature and scope of many workplaces as well as cultural differences. Keep in mind that demographics don't tell the whole story. New research suggests that it is not our age but rather our values that drive behavior. In his book *We Are All the Same Age Now: Valuegraphics, The End of Demographic Stereotypes* (Lioncrest Publishing, 2018), author and consultant David Allison warns against using generational stereotypes and labels to promote our differences. Allison conducted more than 500,000 surveys and concluded that individuals may have little in common as a result of birth years but a great deal in common when it comes to what we care about.

Consider this quote from William Gibson, an American-Canadian speculative fiction writer: "The future is already here. It's just not evenly distributed yet." More than 20 years ago, futurists were recognizing that both access and aptitude play a role in democratizing technology. Advances in technology are making communication both easier and more complicated. Much depends on where you are on the learning and adaptation curve.

How to Use This Book

The focus of this book is to help you increase the effectiveness of your communication at work. Perhaps you are a baby boomer adapting to unfamiliar communications technologies as part of your work. You may be a mid-level professional hoping to move into a leadership role, knowing that transferable communication skills are key to advancement. Perhaps you're comfortable using a wide range of digital communication platforms but seek guidance in the best practices related to face-to-face communication or resolving conflicts. This book provides context, tools, real-life examples, and tips for effective personal and professional communication. It directly addresses the role of technology and digital communication tools in the workplace.

The book is divided into two parts. Part 1 focuses on the basic, but critical, communication skills of speaking and writing in both offline and online environments. Part 2 is all about the vital relationship-building skills we need to succeed in today's workplace. Relationship skills are foundational to good communication and are the hallmark of progressive leadership.

Generally, it is most useful to read any book by starting at the beginning and working your way through to the end, but you may have specific areas of immediate concern or interest, so feel free to immerse yourself in any way that best meets your needs. Chapter headings and subheadings are self-explanatory, and each chapter includes a summary list of best practices as well as useful tips and hints.

At the end of the book you will find a self-assessment tool. These are reflective questions designed to help you analyze your personal communication strengths and challenges and increase your self-awareness. Use these in the way that is most useful to you. Perhaps you would like to complete them as you start out so that you can assess as you go, or maybe you would prefer to complete the assessment at the end. It is completely up to you. What matters is that you can identify what works for you and how you can improve your skills.

Let this book act as a road map through the complex world of effective communication in the digital age and allow me to be your guide.

CHAPTER 2

SPEAKING WELL AT WORK

To become an accomplished communicator, it's essential that you first learn to speak well. You may spend much of the working day behind a screen, sending and receiving e-mails, in chat threads with coworkers, preparing documents, or running data. Still, your ability to communicate well verbally, whether in casual coffee time conversations, at meetings, or in more formal settings, will impact your career success. What you say, how you say it, and the words you choose leave a lasting impression on your customers, coworkers, and managers.

Nearly everyone has an example of a time when a spoken message had a huge positive effect. Words of advice and encouragement from a mentor or colleague, the impact of a TED talk, or the influence of a political speech are all examples of the power of speaking well.

It is equally likely that you can think of a time when someone's words had an adverse impact. Reflect on the badly timed, tactless, or inappropriate jokes told at office social gatherings. A poorly delivered pep talk or a monotonous presentation can leave a long-lasting negative impression. If you think about these examples in your own life and work, you can see how important it is to develop good verbal skills.

At work, your ability to thoughtfully articulate your perspectives and opinions, share constructive feedback, and clearly present ideas and concepts will contribute to your success. Words have the power to hurt or to encourage, influence, and motivate. That is why it is imperative that we choose them wisely.

Interactions and Conversations

The rise of digital communication is constantly changing the way we interact. A quick Internet search reveals that we send more than 23 billion texts daily worldwide. The average American can expect to receive up to 94 texts in the course of a typical working day and more than 600 in the course of a week. Sending and receiving texts, direct messages (DMs), and instant messages (IMs) is simple and quick, and given the "instant" nature of the medium, we expect response times to be immediate as well. The form is designed to be short and informal, employing abbreviations and ideograms like emojis to simplify expression. However, while texting is efficient and convenient, it does not replace the need for face-to-face interaction with coworkers, customers, or clients. As we become accustomed to short-form digital communication, it is tempting to replace other, more time-consuming modes of communication with texting or text-speak.

While digital communications have their place at work, speaking and writing well are foundational communication skills, and it is vitally important to develop and hone these. It is well worth the time you invest to convey your message whether you are engaging in casual coffee room conversations, meeting with clients, proposing new ideas, or leading formal presentations.

A couple of years ago, I had the opportunity to work with a young rising star in business. Let's call her Nala. One of the first females to break into the leadership level of her organization, Nala brought not only a much-needed new perspective into the company, she came with many fresh ideas, insightful observations about improvements to processes and systems, and a real enthusiasm for her role. At meetings, she eagerly presented her ideas along with lucid and proactive arguments to support her proposals. Despite the relevance of what she was presenting, she very often left these meetings without achieving her goals. Not only was the organization not adopting her ideas, colleagues were dismissing them. This was frustrating and stressful. By the time we started working together, Nala had entered into adversarial relationships with her peers and was feeling deeply discouraged in her new role.

Through the coaching process, we identified a few key communication issues Nala needed to address. First, she was overcommunicating. She arrived at meetings with her arguments and rationales completely worked out in advance. Her colleagues had no opportunity for real input into the ideas she was proposing. She also tended to take command of the room in meetings, speaking first as a way to assert herself and demonstrate that she was passionate about her role. Nala is an extrovert whose primary communication channel is verbal, and for some of her colleagues, especially the introverts, it was difficult to absorb the amount of information she was presenting. Because coworkers felt overwhelmed, they tended to block her ideas without digesting them.

We devised a strategy where Nala began breaking her ideas down into smaller chunks, presenting them conceptually at first and then listening carefully to the feedback she received. Once she understood her coworkers' specific objections and concerns, Nala was able to address their issues over a series of meetings. Nala had to adapt her style. She needed to exercise patience, curb her enthusiasm, and practice active listening. I also asked her to be sensitive to the communication styles and preferences of others.

We agreed that her colleague, Abe, has a somewhat aggressive, directive style and prefers to oversee discussions. It is important to Abe that coworkers seek his opinion and that he has an opportunity to express it. Nala's approach seemed threatening and excluded him at the outset. Jon is a thoughtful, somewhat passive introvert. While he didn't actively oppose Nala's ideas, he needed more time to process them. As someone who benefits from having a written summary for reference, he felt lost and overstimulated with the amount of information Nala presented at once. Alan is a "big picture" guy, strategic and intuitive. He needed to see how Nala's ideas linked to the company's vision.

By taking the time to review and reflect on her approach and style as well as the approach and styles of her colleagues, Nala was able to repair her damaged relationships and improve her verbal communication skills overall. Today, she holds a senior industry leadership position and is often behind the podium at conferences, seminars, and conventions.

KEEPING IT SIMPLE

In the preceding example, Nala learned the value of breaking her communication into small digestible chunks and listening for feedback before making her complete case. One of her key barriers to success was that she overwhelmed her audience with information. The way to simplify an interaction is to ask yourself: What is the most efficient, best, and most appropriate way I can convey this information? This helps you not only decide the channel to use—a face-to-face conversation, an e-mail communication, or a short text—but it will also help you streamline your message.

While context matters, it is also important to get to the point. Everybody appreciates direct communication, and in the digital age, time and attention are two of our most precious commodities. This doesn't give you permission to be terse, rude, or insensitive. Always consider the audience and be aware of their communications needs and preferences.

In our communications practice we use a simple model when we are crafting messages for client use. The 27-9-3 rule requires you to make your point in no more than 27 words, within a time frame no longer than nine seconds (the average length of a media sound bite), and with no more than three messages or main points. The model is based on research in risk communication, building on the rule of three from Aristotle's *Rhetoric*, an ancient Greek treatise on the art of persuasion. If you apply this model to your spoken and written exchanges, you will find it a powerful tool for clear communication.

Here are some tips for speaking more clearly:

- Organize your thoughts and decide on your main messages. Do you have a beginning, middle, and end? Try to present no more than three main points at a time.
- Get to the point. Be concise and say exactly what you mean.
- Enunciate and don't be afraid to pause, breathe, and repeat your message if necessary.

PAYING ATTENTION TO BODY LANGUAGE

Carol Kinsey Goman is a best-selling author of 12 business books, including *The Silent Language of Leaders: How Body Language Can Help—or Hurt—How You Lead*. Considered an authority on the impact of body language in the workplace, Goman wrote the following in a 2014 Forbes.com article:

> *"In face-to-face meetings our brains process the continual cascade of nonverbal cues that we use as the basis for building trust and professional intimacy. As a communication medium, face-to-face*

interaction is information rich. People are interpreting the meaning of what you say only partially from the words you use. They get most of your message (and all of the emotional nuance behind the words) from vocal tone, pacing, facial expressions and body language. And, consciously or unconsciously, you are processing the instantaneous nonverbal responses of others to help gauge how well your ideas are being accepted."

Let's go back to the Nala example. In her enthusiasm for colleagues to hear her, Nala concentrated her efforts on what she was going to say. One of the things she failed to do was read the room. Had she done so, she would have quickly seen that her coworkers were not engaged. Abe crossed his arms defensively and leaned away in his chair. The eye contact across the table between Jon and Alan, the two department heads most affected by her proposed changes, verged on eye-rolling. Because she was caught up in making verbal arguments and using logic and persuasiveness as her tools, she failed to observe the doodling, shuffling of feet, and checking of smartphones that signaled the checking out of her audience. In our sessions together, I asked her to revisit and recall these unsuccessful meetings and describe what she remembered in terms of physical cues from her coworkers. She was able to accurately recall the body postures, fidgeting, eye-rolling, and other nonverbal cues that coworkers sent across the table. On a subconscious level, all her senses were working. She simply needed to pay attention to the cues, interpret them, and adapt.

Social scientists define body language as the process of communicating nonverbally through conscious or unconscious gestures and movements. This includes eye contact, body posture, gestures, facial expressions, vocal tone, and touch—such as handshakes. Nowhere are we more able to utilize all our senses to assess meaning, create trust, and build rapport than in face-to-face interactions. This points to a significant limitation of digital communication, particularly the nonvisual channels. We may be able to perceive more on a voice call, taking cues from tone of voice and inflection, and video calls offer us the full scope of visual cues, but none of the digital mediums allow for the empathetic nuances available to us in person.

WORKING REMOTELY

The Internet and wireless technology mean that today we can redefine how and where we work. Collaboration and conferencing tools such as Slack, Trello, Asana, Zoom, and Skype free us from brick-and-mortar locations. Virtual or remote teams offer businesses access to global talent and offer employees flexibility and opportunity. However, remote work is not without its challenges.

Working remotely myself, my office is in my backpack. I carry a laptop, tablet, and smartphone with me almost everywhere I go. The upside is that I am available to clients and my projects are at my fingertips, but this is also the downside. Remote workers must create realistic boundaries around work time and have a healthy work-life balance. Teams need to discuss and define the parameters of remote work and be clear about expectations.

Working remotely also poses unique communications challenges, especially for teams. It is difficult to build trust and a culture of collaboration without physical proximity. While social media has helped us develop relationships in virtual space, it still requires effort to sustain these bonds. If your team is global, there may be cultural, language, or time barriers to consider. Deal with these up front and make agreements around how to communicate effectively despite them.

Often those who find remote meetings difficult are those who are easily distractible. They find it hard to bring the required focus and clarity to a meeting without being in the physical presence of their colleagues. Platforms and software will make your job easier, but it is important that you know how to use them. Make sure you receive adequate training and practice using the tools before you go "live." Expect glitches and, when possible, anticipate them.

Here are a few best practices for working remotely:

- Bring the same focus and concentration to digital or remote meetings that you would bring to an in-person meeting. Be fully present.

- Set aside the necessary time, be prepared, and have the tools and resources you need at hand.

- Remove distractions and avoid interruptions (if you have pets or small children, set boundaries and limit their access).

- If you rarely or never meet with your colleagues in person, reach out to them casually via other channels. This will help you establish social bonds and build connections outside the formal meeting setting.

- Remember that if you are teleconferencing without video, you are without visual cues. Listen carefully and ask clarifying questions if necessary.

Public Speaking

Many people find the idea of public speaking terrifying. Nevertheless, good public speaking skills are part of the effective communication toolbox. As you progress through your career, you will likely have to speak in public—whether presenting to large audiences at conferences or to small groups at your office. Some of these opportunities will be in person, where you will be leading a group from the front of the room or from a podium. In other circumstances you may be broadcasting to a group digitally. Developing and fine-tuning your presentation skills will not only help you in these situations, but will also help you run or participate in meetings effectively.

For many years I designed and delivered public speaking workshops to clients in sectors from government to industry. I developed a set of principles that I call the five P's of public speaking. These are purpose, preparation, practice, passion, and presentation.

PURPOSE

Before you dive into giving a speech or presentation, ask yourself the following questions:

- What is/are my key message(s)?
- How does this message benefit my audience?
- What are the barriers to people accepting this message?
- In the end, what do I want my audience to do?

Speeches or presentations are designed to inform, educate, inspire, entertain, or enlighten an audience. They are more powerful if there is a persuasive end in mind. Asking yourself what you want the audience to do clarifies your purpose. Your personal reasons for giving presentations may include getting more practice, overcoming barriers, or gaining new skills. Remembering the purpose, both professional and personal, will not only help in planning an effective presentation, but focusing on your key message will help if you start to "lose it" or encounter hostile reactions.

PREPARATION

Once you are clear about the purpose for your presentation or speech, you can prepare the content. Find out as much as you can about the audience.

- What is the audience size, age range, and interest level?
- What are their expectations?
- What common ground do you share with them?
- Where are they positioned about the issues you plan to raise?
- What is their knowledge or experience level?

Find out if participants know one another and how well. This affects the dynamics in the group. As you prepare your speech or outline, check your purpose. Are you capturing the key messages? Will the audience relate? Find out what you can about the facility or the room you will be using. Consider using PowerPoint slides, video, audio, or other technologies to support your presentation and make it more interesting. Check and test the technology. Can you arrange the physical environment to suit you and the audience? Looking after these details in advance will enable you to focus on the content of your presentation and set you up for success. Remember the old saying: "If you fail to prepare, you prepare to fail."

PRACTICE

To become good at anything takes practice. Few great presenters are born that way. Experience creates self-confidence. Practice at home, use friends or family members as rehearsal audiences, and obtain their feedback. If you are presenting on behalf of a team, enlist their support as a test audience. A personal coach can also help. Regular practice with a professional may be worth the investment if public speaking is part of your career path.

PASSION

The late Maya Angelou, a renowned author and activist, said, "I've learned that people will forget what you said, people will forget what you did, but people will never forget how you made them feel." The most important factor in successful public speaking is making an emotional connection with your group. Your energy and passion for the topic (or lack of them) will be tangible to the audience. Even if your topic is dry, find something, no matter how insignificant it might seem, that "grabs" you and build your speech or presentation around it. People connect with a speaker who speaks with passion.

These principles apply in preparing to lead or participate in a meeting. Know the purpose for the meeting and your role in it. Research other attendees and understand their positions. Prepare materials in advance, and if you are leading a section of the meeting, practice. Obtain feedback from your team or supportive colleagues. Pay attention to your energy and enthusiasm level for the meeting topic. Adjust as needed. If you are broadcasting to a group digitally, clarity of purpose and message matter, and you need to be meticulous in preparing and practicing with your technical equipment. Now, let's move on to our final of the five P's: presentation.

PRESENTATION

Several factors contribute to the effectiveness of any presentation. While content matters, an audience responds to not only what you say, but how you say it. Tone of voice, volume, and body language all convey your message. Nonverbal cues are important, so pay attention to how you look and what you wear, whether you sit or stand, how you move, and the gestures you use. The two most important parts of your presentation are the first 30 and last 15 seconds. During this crucial time, work to capture the audience's attention and hold it. Make eye contact. In a digital presentation, looking at the camera is the equivalent of making eye contact with your audience. In all cases, start and finish with a strong message.

The surest way to command a room is to speak with conviction. People can tell when a presenter lacks confidence or is disingenuous. Be yourself and show your sincerity, passion, and enthusiasm for the topic. Be engaged and candid. Audiences will "check out" (leave the room mentally) if a speaker is insincere or condescending. You can demonstrate conviction through body language, facial expressions, and eye contact. This will be effective even in a cross-cultural context where language may be a barrier. Sincerity will always outperform flamboyance.

Be creative. How can you make your presentation as interesting as possible? Use visuals like slides or video to enhance your material. Tell stories using personal anecdotes and examples. Use humor, especially if it comes naturally, but avoid opening with a joke. This can easily flop. Humor should always be appropriate. If you have any doubt about the suitability of a joke or story, *do not use it.* For many years I worked with politicians, and our mantra for speeches was "If in doubt, leave it out."

Check in with your audience periodically, even if it is a large one, and ask them questions. Watch for reactions (which will largely be nonverbal) and adjust as needed. If you think you are starting to "lose it," breathe, make eye contact with a friendly face, check your notes or slides, and don't panic. The audience wants you to succeed.

One of the key errors that inexperienced presenters make is the failure to use silence as a tool in the presentation. Pausing for questions and leaving adequate time allows people to formulate their responses before rushing on to the next subject. Many people require time to mentally process and will appreciate pauses in your presentation to digest information. Inexperienced speakers feel they must keep talking at any cost. This can also be a function of ego. Some speakers are personally uncomfortable with silence, but it's an excellent tool to elicit ideas that sometimes lie at the edge of the comfort zone. With practice you will become more comfortable with holding silence in the room. Presenting is like anything else—the more experience you have, the easier it becomes.

A NOTE ABOUT NERVES

Nerves can manifest themselves in several, mostly unpleasant, ways. By understanding the physiology behind nervousness, we can understand how and why we react the way we do in pressure situations. Speaking in public is a high-pressure situation; it is a live performance with no rewind button.

This kind of pressure sets up a reaction in the body. The situation is perceived as a threat. Human beings, as with all creatures in the natural world, are equipped with instinctive defenses that come into play when we think we are threatened. It is important to realize that this means not that we actually *are* threatened but that we *perceive* a threat. When we experience fear, the body sends adrenaline into the system to provide us with the strength and energy we need to protect ourselves—to fight, to flee, or to freeze. Adrenaline charges through the system and our bodies react.

The key message here is that *nervousness is only energy.* We need energy in order to create a dynamic, interesting presentation. In long sessions, the presenter's energy sets the tone and level for the participants. The ability to maintain a consistent energy level is critical to maintain the groups' interest. In live theatre, directors often instruct actors to "hold the energy" or "up the energy." This enables them to keep their performances sparkling and rivet the audience to the stage. Problems with energy occur when it is bottled up. If we are particularly keyed up about a situation, the energy in the system builds up and has to release somehow. This is when we begin to see the interesting manifestations of nerves, such as stuttering, shaking, nausea, dropping things, freezing, or blanking out.

One of the secrets to coping with nerves is to muster the energy to move. By playing with your energy levels prior to your presentation, you can spill off excess bottled energy that causes some of the unpleasant reactions but maintain enough energy to "hold the room."

Some suggestions include:

• deep breathing

• physical activity in the evening or a few hours before the presentation

• opera-like singing aloud, making loud vocal noises

• shaking the body or stamping the feet

Remember that practice builds confidence. With more experience, you will become better able to cope with nervousness.

DIGITAL CONFERENCING

Teleconferencing and videoconferencing are rapidly becoming commonplace. Using this technology often means less time and travel on the road and more access to global and remote expertise. During a crisis, such as the 2020 pandemic, it enabled thousands to work remotely. While digital conferencing does not replace face-to-face engagement, it can be very effective. If geography is an issue, your entire team or work group may meet via teleconferencing, or you may simply invite one or two experts to contribute to an in-person meeting.

I conduct a big part of my corporate consulting and coaching work via teleconference and videoconference. In a typical teleconference, attendees connect using a dial-in number and a numeric code to access the virtual meeting room. The host uses a separate code to ensure that the meeting room is "open" and greets attendees as they arrive. A notification signal beeps or pings as each new person enters the room. If the host is late, attendees are put on hold in a virtual waiting room until the host arrives.

A key piece of etiquette in a teleconference is to identify yourself when you enter the call and as you speak. As the conversation ebbs and flows, you cannot be certain that people will recognize your voice. You also do not have the visual cues and body language that help confer and interpret meaning. You can infer from vocal tone and inflection, but it's helpful to offer other cues in your conversation. An example: "This is Vicki, and I'm smiling as you say that. I'm glad to hear the project is going well."

As with any other meeting, be on time and be prepared. If you are at home or on the road, find a quiet spot and use a good-quality phone. Minimize outside distractions. If you are using a smartphone, use a headset or earbuds and mic. Stay within good range of cell service. You can use a landline speakerphone for listening, but use a handset or a headset with a mic to speak, as the audio quality of most speakerphones is quite poor.

Most conference rooms will be furnished with equipment that is adequate for the size of the room. Make sure that you place microphones near the primary speakers and that they are away from projector fans and that other devices are not blocking them.

Videoconferencing provides us with the rich visual cues that are missing in e-mail, text, or teleconferencing. Most videoconferencing platforms offer screen-sharing solutions that enable meeting participants to collaborate on project documentation, something that is not possible in a teleconference. It is a good alternative to either in-person meetings or teleconferencing, combining live video feeds with screen sharing for group collaboration. This allows remote meeting participants to engage in meaningful real-time face-to-face engagement. Certainly, the social distancing adopted in response to the 2020 coronavirus pandemic accelerated the use of this technology not only for remote work, but also to sustain vital personal connections with family and friends.

TIPS AND TRICKS FOR VIDEO CALLS

A few small considerations specific to videoconferencing go a long way in preparing for your success with them. Here are some of my tips:

- Set up and test your equipment (camera, microphone, speakers) prior to the meeting.

- Be mindful of your facial expressions and gestures. Body language comes into play in videoconference, so use it to your advantage.

- Dress appropriately. Treat your home or hotel room as an extension of the office.

- As with any other meeting, be on time and be prepared.

- With most videoconferencing, you can see yourself as well as other attendees on the screen. Look at the camera and at other attendees, not at yourself. When you look at the camera, it appears that you are looking directly at other individuals in the conference.

- Be aware of the camera view. Adjust the camera so it is at eye level.

- Lighting matters. Natural light is best, but there are many inexpensive LED lights available.

- Use a dedicated audio feed, if possible. Most laptop speakers and microphones are not adequate for clearly communicating via videoconference.

- Be mindful of your background. If you are at home, don't make others look at your laundry pile or unfinished household tasks. It's distracting and unprofessional.

- Limit multitasking to what you might do in an in-person meeting—for example, sipping on a beverage or taking notes by hand. If you start eating, checking e-mail, or using a smartphone, remember that others can see you.

- Minimize distractions, including those that children, pets, and ambient noise generate.

- Ask those who are not speaking to mute their microphones while they listen. This will minimize background noise.

One challenge of multiple video feeds is bandwidth. You may find that you need to exit your video and revert to an audio conference if you have problems with streaming. It helps to prepare a backup option for this scenario.

High-Stakes Conversations

Whether you are delivering a difficult message, asking or answering sensitive questions, or dealing with misunderstandings or unwanted behavior, high-stakes conversations or situations are where the outcome carries weight, because of either the potential risk or reward. Examples include conversations related to:

- compensation
- work performance
- roles and responsibilities
- interpersonal conflict
- harassment, bullying, or abuse*

High-stakes conversations may also concern the success or failure of the business or organization, such as conversations with investors, partners, or strategic alliances. Usually in these cases, the conversation is more formal and includes a presentation, pitch, or proposal. The skills you develop during interpersonal high-stakes conversations will also serve you in these instances. Here are some tips to help you navigate challenging conversations:

Be clear about the purpose of the conversation. What is the real issue? Is there a desired outcome or specific resolution that you need? Think about this in advance and be direct about addressing the actual issue.

Create a safe space and allow adequate time. Most of these conversations will take place face-to-face, and it's important that they are in a private area, free of interruption. Ensure that all parties have time to adequately deal with the issue and that you have agreement to proceed.

Practice self-regulation and manage your emotions. Be as calm as possible going into the exchange. Don't attempt to have a difficult conversation when you are stressed, angry, hungry, or tired. Try not to be defensive or take things personally. Maintain positivity.

Tune into your intuition. You will know if you or others need to say more in a difficult conversation. Be fully present, use your powers of observation, and gently probe for more information.

Be direct. Get to the core of the issue at hand and be sure to deal with facts and evidence rather than interpretation and perception.

Don't make assumptions. Ask questions to clarify issues and confirm mutual understanding before coming to conclusions. Phrases like "Can you say a little more about that . . ." or "Did you mean . . . " can help you dig deeper. Remember that silence can be a tool to allow elusive information to emerge.

__Note:__ In these instances, understand your rights. If someone is harassing, bullying, or abusing you in the workplace, contact your human resources department or a legal representative.

CHOOSING THE CHANNEL: DIGITAL VERSUS IN PERSON

Choose digital when:

- the communication is task- or project-focused or issues are minor.
- you are working fully remotely.
- there are geographic considerations that make it challenging to bring the team together.

- other practical factors or circumstances prevent you from meeting face-to-face.
- flexibility is important.

Choose in person when:

- building trust, creating an emotional connection, or being empathetic matters.
- the stakes are high.
- problems are thorny, subtle, or nuanced.
- discussion would benefit from a synergistic give-and-take.
- you need to establish or repair social bonds.

In a 2018 article on Forbes.com, Carol Kinsey Goman, the expert we met earlier in this chapter, had this to say:

> *"In the midst of a digital age, I believe that face-to-face is still the most productive and powerful communication medium. An in-person meeting offers the best opportunity to engage others with empathy and impact. It builds and supports positive professional connections that we can't replicate in a virtual environment."*

Consider the impact and engagement you hope to have and then choose your channel wisely.

CHAPTER 3

WRITING WELL AT WORK

In today's world, writing by hand using pen and paper seems almost quaint. Many schools no longer teach children cursive writing or penmanship. However, despite the decline in actual writing by hand, we rely on written communication more than ever before, as it the chief method by which we communicate in the digital environment. Whether you are composing a tweet, post, or e-mail, you are using the basic writing skills of composition, sentence structure, grammar, and punctuation. You are making choices about tone, active or passive voice, and audience.

According to Steven Roger Fischer in his book *The History of Writing*, written language "is the single most important and far-reaching technology available to humans and has served as the foundation for virtually all other information technologies from early etchings in clay to the world of digital access that we enjoy today." Writing has been and continues to be an essential component in human communication, development, and progress.

The contemporary workplace requires you to use writing skills for daily correspondence such as e-mail, memos, and texts and for more formal business communications such as reports, proposals, or presentations. The business world often requires you to "put it in writing"—establishing a permanent record of key transactions and strategies and ongoing professional documentation of organizational projects, initiatives, and related data.

To be an effective written communicator, you must learn and understand the basics of good writing craft and navigate the many forms that writing takes, both online and offline.

Leveling Up Your Writing Skills in the Office

Good writing, whether long or short form, is clear, concise, coherent, and specific. The tone of writing for business should be friendly yet professional. Short forms of writing, such as texting, tweeting, and posting on social media, usually are more informal in tone. These mediums are also more personal. Reports, proposals, letters, guides, and manuals are more formal and impersonal.

When writing for business, ask yourself: How formal or informal is the correspondence? Your tone will be different sending colleagues an invitation for lunch versus sending a similar invitation to a client. The first step in deciding what to write and how to write it is identifying the audience. Business writing tends to fall into four categories:

Informational. These are the reports, summaries, agendas, minutes of meetings, and other written data that comprise the organization's essential records. This type of writing generally captures discussions, decisions, and task assignments as well as creates a record for legal or other contractual purposes.

Instructional. Think of manuals and guides, technical documents, and memos. This type of writing provides the reader with the necessary instructions to complete a task or breaks down a set of processes into steps.

Persuasive. Persuasive business writing is especially important to master if you are in sales and marketing or if you are looking to influence decisions. The goal of persuasive writing is to convey information and to convince readers to take some kind of action or sway their perspective. Think of proposals, press releases, newsletters (which can also be informational), sales content, or presentations. Promotional writing is a form of persuasive writing.

Transactional. Consider this the necessary day-to-day correspondence for your company or organization to conduct business. This is the free flow of e-mails, announcements, and reminders that comprise everyday communication in the office.

The next step is determining the goal for your writing. What is the purpose of the communication? This will also help with style and tone. What is the goal of this communication? If you cannot identify a clear purpose for the communication, ask yourself if it is really necessary. Our inboxes are crowded enough. If there is not a clear and compelling reason to communicate in writing, save yourself and the potential recipient from wasted time.

Good writing requires discipline. This means concentration and focus, two things in short supply in the age of distractions. Concentration involves the ability to focus your attention or thought to a single activity—in this case, putting your words on the page. Focus is about finding the center of interest, or central theme, and narrowing your attention. At work, there are multiple tasks competing for your time and attention. You will need to carve out time to properly focus on your written work.

You can consolidate an efficient writing process into three segments—inventing, drafting, and revising. Typically inventing comprises about 30% of writing time, during which you generate and focus your ideas or main arguments and consider the context—audience, purpose, and form. The drafting process enables you to put words on the page, taking you one step closer to a finished product. This should be about 20% of your writing time. You will spend the remaining 50% of writing time in revision—editing, deleting, substituting, and rearranging text. Keeping your audience and purpose in mind, revise for accuracy, context, paragraph and sentence structure, spelling, grammar, and punctuation.

For several months, my team and I wrote and produced a quarterly newsletter for one of our major clients. Devin, a relatively new member of their communications team, asked to take on the newsletter as an in-house project. We worked with Devin to generate topic ideas and to develop an annual editorial calendar. We also provided a graphic template and brand identity guidelines. During the transition quarter, we checked in several times to see if Devin needed any assistance or help in planning editorial content, drafting sections, or proofreading. He assured us and other members of the team that the newsletter was "on the list" and that he did not require any input or assistance.

Devin's first newsletter was an epic failure. It fell short not only in terms of meaningful content and visual appeal, it was poorly written and full of spelling and other errors. There were two crucial blunders on Devin's part. The first was that he simply neglected to give himself adequate time to do a good job. He overestimated his own writing and editing ability and underestimated the actual time needed. The second was that he failed to collaborate. It is extremely difficult to edit your own writing. In business, unless the correspondence is confidential, your writing will benefit from a second (or third!) pair of eyes. You must set your ego aside and enlist the help of others, particularly if the stakes are high.

Today, Devin is part of a three-person newsletter team that bounces ideas around, creates shared content, and carefully vets each edition of the newsletter. This process is not without its challenges, but it does ensure a better, more professional product.

SIX SIMPLE QUESTIONS TO GUIDE YOUR WRITING

One of the best tools to use when inventing, drafting, or revising your written content, and one that you can apply to any form of writing, is the 5Ws and H series of questions. Elementary school teachers may have introduced this model to you, as it is a fundamental way to teach writing composition skills. Journalistic or investigative reporters use it widely for fact-finding. A solid news story covers these six elements, and effective business writing does, too. You can use this series of questions in several ways. Some examples are listed here:

Who:

- Who is the audience?

- Who is in charge?

- Who is affected?

- Who made the decision?

What:

- What is the subject/topic?

- What does it mean?

- What information is needed?

- What's in it for me/them?

- What is the decision?

- What else should the reader know?

When:

- When will/does/did this take place?

- When will there be more information?

- When are the deadlines?

Where:

- Where will/does/did this take place?
- Where are the affected locations?
- Where can I find more information?
- Where did the information/decision originate?

Why:

- Why does this matter to the reader/company/staff?
- Why is this the right/wrong decision/approach?
- Why now?

How:

- How was the decision made?
- How will the problem be solved?
- How will actions/changes take place?
- How will information flow?
- How does it impact the reader?

In my work with this model, I add another W: Want. This W is especially useful in negotiations, persuasive writing, when crafting a call to action, to clarify requests, or if you are looking for redress in your work. What do you **want** the reader to do? What do you **want** out of the transaction? Using the 5Ws and H model when you are in the inventing phase of writing will help you focus on the important aspects of your message. You can also use it to review your communication to ensure that it is complete.

SELF-EDITING FOR CLARITY AND BREVITY

One of the advantages of written communication over face-to-face or telephone interaction is that it allows the receiver of the information time to contemplate and absorb the message before composing a reply. However, digital messaging infers a sense of urgency that is inherent in the platforms. Although the etiquettes vary—a longer response time is more acceptable when e-mailing than when texting, for example—we are in an age where response times are short and people value brevity. We simply do not have the time or the inclination to read and decipher lengthy or convoluted messages. Conveying your message clearly and concisely without sacrificing quality is a skill you must develop. Attention span issues aside, people are more likely to read, understand, and act upon concise messages. Here are a few tips to help you:

Keep it concise. Remember the 27-9-3 rule we discussed in chapter 2? It also applies to writing. Try to make your written point(s) less than 27 words long with no more than three main messages per correspondence.

Keep it clear. Apply the 5Ws and H. Check your messages to see if you have covered the important information. These will vary depending on what you are communicating.

Keep it professional. Proofread! Grammar, punctuation, and spelling matter in every written exchange including presentation slides, reports, e-mails, texts, and instant messages. Each has different protocols and etiquettes, but language rules matter.

A note about abbreviations. Abbreviations, contractions, initialisms, symbols, and acronyms are all shortened forms of writing. Typically, protocol is to abbreviate social and professional titles such as *Mr., Mrs., Ms., Dr.,* or *Rev.* in nearly all forms of correspondence. Common business abbreviations include *CC:, encl.,*

RSVP, P.S., Faqs, and *FYI.* In general, you can safely abbreviate days of the week, months of the year, and geographic locations. Acronyms tend to represent jargon that is industry specific. *TOC* stands for "table of contents" if you are a writer, "theory of computation" if you are a computer scientist, and "technical operations center" if you are police or paramilitary. As long as the respective workplace employees understand these abbreviations, use acronyms freely in internal messages. Avoid using them in external communication where people can easily misunderstand them. Remember that the abbreviations and slang commonly used in texts do not translate well into other writing forms. Keep in mind that SMS abbreviations are not necessarily universally understood.

GENERATION GAPS IN THE WORKPLACE

Earlier in this book, we discussed the generations in terms of their categories related to birth years, from Centennials to Millennials to baby boomers. Here's another perspective. Ray Wang in his book *Disrupting Digital Business* defines digital generations by the way they approach technology. We wrote about these in *Digital Legacy Plan.* They include the following:

- "digital natives," who have known digital all their lives and willingly embrace all digital opportunities for work and play

- "digital immigrants," who by choice or by requirement have transitioned from analog to digital

- "digital voyeurs," who are aware of digital and accept its existence but have not yet joined the digital ranks

- "digital holdouts," or those who are content with their non-digital existence and resist and even fear any shift toward a more digital life

- the "digitally disengaged," who have tried digital and have stopped using it. They are disillusioned by the broken promises of privacy and access.

Wang's approach points us toward the digital skills gap that can exist between the generations but may also exist simply based on adaptation no matter what your age. You can bridge the gap by choosing the communication channels that are most likely to reach colleagues in a given generation or with a given skill set. In coaching, we call this "meeting them where they are." It is also helpful not to make assumptions about digital skills based solely on age and stage.

Writing Effectively for Digital Communication

Chris Brogan is a *New York Times* best-selling author and president of Chris Brogan Media. He is a thoughtful, articulate, and ethical digital strategist and advisor who has been spotting trends in the digital space and working with clients like Disney, Google, and Microsoft for decades. He sends out a useful biweekly e-newsletter, one of the few I read regularly.

In one, titled "Communication—It's Already Changed," Brogan essentially announces the demise of long-form writing.

Brogan's insights resonated because we do considerable business writing in our company. We coordinate communications and marketing efforts for customers, and we're forever urging them to focus and keep things short. This is especially true in digital communications, where increasingly the world is in a "smartphone first" context. Here, slightly paraphrased, are the points Brogan asks us to consider:

- People aren't reading as much—only 19 minutes a day.
- Language is shifting—from "conversational" to "informal"; from "formerly offensive" to "f-word acceptable"; from "in depth" to "as brief as possible."
- Visuals are more and more core to everyday language.
- Brevity. It's even more brief (like Facebook Messenger brief).
- Multi-touch communication across a variety of platforms is more the norm than "that one place I know I can reach them" communication.

Brogan is right. Communication and the way we use language *have* changed. To write effectively for digital communication, we must strike a balance between the relaxed tone and style of the online world and professional accuracy and clarity.

Are you familiar with the term *business casual*? We frequently use it to describe the mode of dress at networking or other business events. It sounds like an oxymoron, but it describes the middle path we need to find in digital business writing. Today's business writing is a form of business casual for words.

The length of written communication has also changed. E-mail and text messaging lend themselves to smaller, more clearly written segments. Social media has contributed to the shrinking of written forms. Twitter, which launched with a 140-character limit, has influenced the way we convey our messages. Writing must be even more precise and yet still descriptive. Written digital communication takes place on devices, and we are left without the auditory, visual, and other cues available in verbal or face-to-face communication, so we must rely on language itself and ideograms such as emojis to help convey nuances and subtlety.

E-MAIL

The most common form of daily business communication is e-mail. Worldwide, we send roughly 293 billion e-mails per day! Think about your own workday. How many e-mails do you estimate you send and receive? For most workplaces e-mail is the backbone of internal communication and the primary means of connection. Learning to craft effective messages and manage your inbox is an important business skill.

As a digital medium, we could classify e-mail as a less formal mode of communication, but business e-mails remain very different in tone and structure than those you send casually to a friend or family member. Business e-mails should contain greetings and signatures and be concise, clear, and grammatically correct. By their nature, they are intended to be brief, but e-mails must contain the important information you are trying to convey.

Here is an example from an e-mail exchange. Remember Devin? Devin's boss assigned him to a new event planning team tasked with introducing and hosting large-scale stakeholder events. Carole was an outside event planning expert leading the team, and Devin's role was to provide administrative and clerical support. The team launched into the project, and deadlines loomed. Carole sent the following e-mail:

TO: Devin

SUBJECT: Question

Hey Devin,

Is it possible to get a geographic breakdown of event attendees, along with their work unit assignment numbers?

Thx so much!

C

Devin's reply:

> TO: Carole
>
> SUBJECT: re: Question
>
> Yes

The problem with this communication is obvious. Devin's one-word reply, while an accurate response to the question, doesn't address Carole's actual request and borders on rudeness. We can infer that Carole would like the breakdown provided, and if Devin isn't sure, a more appropriate response would be "Yes, I can provide that to you. When do you need it?" More proactively, he could run the breakdown and reply with the needed document attached. In this example, both Devin and Carole are under-communicating. Carole needs to be more specific, both in her subject line and in her request. Carole's tone is quite casual, belying the potential urgency of the message. Here is a better-framed e-mail:

> TO: Devin
>
> SUBJECT: ACTION REQUIRED: Breakdown of Event Attendees
>
> Hello Devin,
>
> Is it possible to get a geographic breakdown of event attendees, along with their work unit assignment numbers? If so, please send it to me as soon as possible. If not, please call me to discuss options. Thank you!
>
> Cheers, Carole

HOW TO WRITE BETTER E-MAILS

With the dozens of e-mails we send and receive on a daily basis, it's worth taking the time to improve your e-mail writing skills. Here are my top tips:

Effective Subject Lines

We sort, prioritize, and scan multitudes of e-mails daily. An effective subject line provides a clear and specific summary of the subject of the message and conveys relative urgency. Take a quick scan of your own inbox. How many of the subject lines clearly communicate the message? Think of subject lines like news headlines. You want to tell the recipient what the e-mail is about and capture their attention, especially if the matter is urgent or requires action. Adding ACTION REQUIRED to the subject line (as in the preceding e-mail) is a good example of how to do so.

Greetings and Signatures

Use professional greetings such as *Dear*, *Hello*, or *Good morning/afternoon* and include the recipient's name. *Hey, Jane!* conveys casualness and is more appropriate for personal correspondence or subjects that lack urgency. Use a professional signature that includes your first and last name, job title, department, and company. Avoid using signoffs that are too formal. *Sincerely*, *Kind regards*, and *Respectfully* are old-fashioned. *Thank you*, *Thanks again*, *Cheers*, and *Have a good [day/weekend]* are all acceptable. Always keep the audience in mind.

Body of the E-mail

As with all written communication, review to see if you have included the 5Ws and H. Read the e-mail out loud to yourself to check tone and clarity. Keep it brief. Use paragraph breaks and *do not bury the lede.* Get to the primary purpose of the e-mail as quickly as possible. Be friendly, but don't clutter the e-mail with excessive personal observations and chitchat. Always check your e-mail for spelling, grammar, and punctuation prior to sending. For example, carelessly leaving out the word *not* in the following sentence could have disastrous consequences: "You must not send these documents to CompetiCo."

How and When to Use CC:, BCC:, Reply All:

Confusion reigns when it comes to determining the best etiquette for these fields in e-mail correspondence. Typically, we use CC to include those who need to know about the conversation but are not required to take direct action on the e-mail's content. Using it as a form of FYI is not effective, as those CCed may not always read the e-mail. If you are using CC for FYI, instead cut and paste the content and send it as an FYI e-mail. Do not use CC to CYA—in other words, do not CC/BCC to someone's boss unless there is a compelling reason to do so or CC your own boss to "check" your content unless requested to do so.

There are two interpretations for BCC. It stands for blind carbon copy, and it's a way of sending an e-mail where the primary recipient does not see who else you have copied. A good reason to use this is to protect the BCC recipients' privacy and prevent their inclusion in unnecessary Reply Alls. A poor reason is using BCC to "secretly" include someone in an otherwise private e-mail conversation. This is ethically dubious. If you feel that others need to see the private correspondence, simply forward it to them as a direct and private message with a note as to why. We also use BCC to indicate that the recipient only needs to read the first message but not be included in reply threads. This is a less well-known use of BCC and is easy to misinterpret.

Use Reply All sparingly, especially if the response is not germane to the required task or action. This includes unnecessary replies such as thank you, see you there, or message received. Always think twice before hitting Reply All. Let's keep our inboxes as clutter free as possible.

INSTANT MESSAGING

The use of instant messaging (IM) in the office presents a conundrum. Texting is a very common form of communication today. It is fast becoming the most popular communication channel for mobile users, and many organizations use texting to transact business with customers and clients. By its nature texting is informal and personal, which contradicts the nature of most business communication despite an overall shift to less formality in business exchanges. Nevertheless, instant messaging is becoming more widely used in the workplace. There are also a few cases where it makes sense to use personal texting as a form of internal business communication.

One of the organizations with whom my team works uses texting as a way for employees to stay in touch with each other when attending events such as conferences and conventions. It's a quick and easy way to coordinate meetups and check on travel and accommodation arrangements. Similarly, if your organization coordinates events and activities offsite, texting is a practical means of communicating. It is useful for quick queries that require a yes or no answer or sharing simple factoids: "Yes, meeting is 10:00 a.m."

Many companies are adopting tools like Google Chat and Slack, which are essentially large chat rooms allowing you to organize company communications by channels within the platform. Employees chat via instant messaging within these channels. As employees become accustomed to using these tools, extending that habit into instant messaging or texting outside the platform is a natural next step. Within internal chat rooms it is important to practice professional etiquette. Stay on topic, be friendly, and don't hijack chat threads with personal distractions. Be aware of the conversational culture at your workplace and emulate it.

Given the casualness and immediacy of personal texting, it is not ideally suited to business communications. Unless they are very simple, most responses to business questions require at least some time and thought. If you are using texting as a form of business communication, you will want to communicate to the sender that you will not be responding immediately to complicated questions via text or IM. Here are a few other tips to help you use instant messaging or texting in the office:

Be mindful of tone. Be friendly and casual and use a personal style as appropriate, but remember to be professional.

Keep it simple and clear. Be specific and keep messages concise. Texts are intended to be read in a few seconds. Use simple, action-oriented words and vocabulary that everyone can understand.

Be mindful of spelling and punctuation. In typical personal SMS short-form communication, we often omit vowels and punctuation, but do not shorten words in business texting. Check your spelling and grammar and use punctuation.

Don't overuse emojis. Because of their brevity, texts can be misinterpreted easily. Emojis help convey emotional nuances, but use them sparingly in business texts. (See the next section for more detail about using emojis in a business context.)

Respect preferences. If you know a colleague is not comfortable using text messaging as a form of communication, use other channels such as e-mail.

Consider data ownership. Note that your employer can monitor your activities on any work device. Laws are still evolving around workplace device use and data ownership. It is better to be safe than sorry.

WHEN IS IT OKAY TO USE EMOJIS?

We've discussed how nonverbal cues such as tone of voice, body language, and facial expression can alter how we perceive speech. A significant limitation of communication via text, e-mail, posts, and tweets is the inability to express nuances and offer cues. Emojis (a tiny picture of something) or emoticons (a sequence of characters that represents a facial expression) evolved in part to address this limitation. Emojis can be an easy, fun, and effective way to add nuance to your messages, but etiquettes around their use in business environments are still in flux. Like other forms of communication, we can also misunderstand emoji speak. A smiley face can denote happiness or satisfaction, but it can also denote sarcasm. The receiver still has to determine the symbol's meaning.

Look at your own message threads or e-mail inbox. How are your colleagues and coworkers using emojis? What about your clients? How do you respond to them when you see them in messages? Are you always clear about their meaning and usefulness?

Even though business communication is becoming more casual, we have not yet adopted all the quirks of personal communication into the business vernacular. Emojis are a kind of digital slang. A good question to ask is: Will adding an emoji make this communication clearer? I am not averse to adding a smiley face, winky face, or heart icon to my business communication, especially if I think it will enhance the meaning. It is also consistent with my personal brand. Here are a few tips if you plan to use emojis in your business communication:

- Stick to emojis or emoticons that express positive emotional states. A "thumbs down" or "frowny face" has a negative connotation and therefore leaves a negative impression.

- Use emojis that express universally understood facial expressions or hand gestures rather than other symbols. According to emojitracker.com, facial expressions are the most commonly used symbols.

- Do not use emojis to replace actual words. Think of them more as an embellishment to the tone of your core message.

- Use them in moderation—usually no more than two in any message; know your audience and consider the form. Emojis definitely do not belong in proposals and reports, but they can have a place in instant or text messages and occasional e-mails.

E-MAIL ETIQUETTE

Managing Your Inbox

An overflowing inbox can be overwhelming. It becomes like a to-do list that you never tackle, contributing to stress and frustration. If possible, set aside regular times in your daily work schedule to deal with e-mail.

You don't have to answer every e-mail immediately. Response times will vary depending on the communication's urgency and its related impacts. As a general rule, if an e-mail requires no action from you, either delete it or archive it. If the action or response required is simple, deal with it as soon as it comes in and then archive it. If the response requires more time and thought, then save or "snooze" the message with a dated reminder to yourself to respond. Notify the sender that you have received the message and tell them when you will respond.

Your company may have a response time policy. If not, a good practice is to respond to members of your team the same day, as you rely on one another to be productive. For others in the organization, generally 24 hours is acceptable unless the message is urgent or time-sensitive. For those outside the organization, they can generally wait two to three days, depending on the urgency. Try to deal with all e-mails by the end of each week.

One Subject, One E-mail

Take the time to gather your thoughts and be clear about the main points of your communication. Limit your e-mail to one subject. If you have several points on the same subject, try to include them in the same e-mail rather than sending a succession of e-mails. If you are writing with more than one or two queries, or actions, number them. Also let the recipient know. For example: "Good morning, Devin, I am writing to ask you three things . . . "

Choose Your Words Carefully

Write only what you would say to someone face-to-face. Never send anything offensive, insulting, or intimate from your business address. Conveying tone is very difficult via e-mail. Avoid using negative phrasing or sarcasm and use adjectives sparingly. Avoid using emojis or emoticons unless they are very simple or positive (e.g., smiley face, thumbs-up). DO NOT USE ALL CAPS in the body text. It looks like shouting.

Professional E-mail Address

Use a professional e-mail address. Your company will assign a work e-mail address to you as an employee. Avoid sending work-related e-mails from your home address. It may be a breach of company confidentiality or policy, and it looks unprofessional. When working remotely, take the time to sign into your official e-mail account. Keep personal and professional e-mail addresses separate.

FROM A3 TO ZZZ: COMMON DIGITAL TERMS NOT USED IN PERSON

There are literally hundreds, if not thousands, of text and chat letter or numeric abbreviations. In a short online search for this section, I came up with more than 1,500, from A3 ("anytime, anywhere, anyplace") to ZZZ ("sleeping or bored"). I've listed some of the common SMS abbreviations that you might run into in a business setting and their translations here. There are many hundreds more that you may come across. If you don't understand them, a simple Internet search is your friend. Look them up or ask the sender to clarify.

AFC	away from computer
AKA	also known as
ASAP	as soon as possible
BRB	be right back
CTA	call to action
EOD	end of day
EOM	end of message
FOMO	fear of missing out
FYI	for your information
ICYMI	in case you missed it
IDK	I don't know
IMO	in my opinion
JK (J/K)	just kidding
JOMO	joy of missing out

LMK	let me know
LOL	laughing out loud
NRN	no reply necessary
NSFW	not safe for work
OOTO (OOO)	out of the office
OT	off topic
ROI	return on investment
SFW	safe for work
TL;DR	too long didn't read
TTYL(S)	talk to you later (soon)
YTD	year to date

In the context of how written communication has changed, TL; DR is particularly interesting. It is used as a response to a wall of text you received (or sent) or to an especially long and detailed document to indicate that you didn't read it; it can also be used to signal a short brief or summary of a longer, more detailed document to follow the TL;DR synopsis. Generally, if you receive a TL; DR reply, you need to include a short summary.

While some of these abbreviations have been in use for many years in business, such as ASAP, FYI, and YTD, many more are coming into popular use as a spillover from texting and computerspeak. Nevertheless, SMS language is a casual form. Consider the context, audience, corporate culture, and medium before choosing to use them in business communication.

CHAPTER 4

PUTTING WRITING AND SPEAKING SKILLS TO THE TEST

You will never run short of opportunities to practice speaking and writing skills in your day-to-day work. There will also be instances, either formal or informal, where asserting these skills can make a significant difference in your career trajectory. In this chapter we'll look at applying what you are learning to a few real-life scenarios—including networking events, workplace negotiations, and writing effective proposals or reports.

Networking

We've all been to networking events where sharp-eyed people circle the room like sharks, pressing business cards into hands and becoming dismissive if it seems there's no sale to be had. This approach gives networking a bad name and discourages many from taking advantage of its benefits. Networking provides an opportunity to generate leads, acquire clients, and sell products. These, however, are secondary objectives. The first and primary purpose of networking is to build relationships. An old marketing adage is that we do business with people we know, like, and trust. People cannot come to like and trust you without getting to know you first.

If you are just starting out in your career, the contacts and professional connections that you make now may become relationships that serve you for a lifetime. If you are moving up the corporate ladder, your company will expect you to be an ambassador, attending events and representing the business or organization officially or unofficially.

When my business was new, I attended many networking events and volunteered for community events and committees. I have a strong community service ethic, but I also wanted people to know about me and my business. One of my early volunteer stints resulted in our company acquiring a client that has stayed with us for nearly two decades and continues to refer us to many other valuable clients.

PREPARING FOR A NETWORKING EVENT

One of the first questions to ask yourself before a networking event is: What is the compelling reason for me to attend? Having a clear purpose in mind is helpful, both in terms of overcoming nerves and in determining how to use your time at the event.

Networking is difficult for many people, especially for introverts who prefer deep one-to-one conversations to circulating in a crowd making chitchat. Getting together in a room full of strangers to talk about yourself and your work can be daunting. The good news is many people prefer these deeper conversations and are interested in making a real connection, even at large social events. My advice is to go for quality over quantity at networking events.

Here are some of my top tips for better networking:

Look for real connections. Connection means much more than an opportunity to sell and be sold. There is a tendency, resulting in part from Internet sales culture, to think of people as "eyeballs," leads, or prospects. This is a transactional approach.

If building relationships is the primary goal of your networking activity, think of the people you meet as individuals, not transactions, and focus on them one at a time, seeking to connect on a personal level. Don't squander the face-to-face opportunity to engage fully. Make eye contact, pay attention to body language, and practice active listening.

Prepare your elevator pitch. At business events, the conversation will naturally turn to who you are, what you do, and where you work. Refer back to chapter 2 when we talked about the 27-9-3 rule. Come up with a short sound bite that introduces who you are and what you do and includes something interesting about your work or your life. When you meet someone, ask about what they do. Have clean and presentable business cards handy, but don't rush to exchange them. Wait until you've established some common ground. Be sure to give a card to anyone with whom you have agreed to follow up and ask for their card in return.

Make small talk. Take some time to research the event. Most networking groups have an active website that lists members and their industries. This will help you come up with topics of interest to those attending and help you identify desirable connections. Visit their websites and devise one or two specific questions to ask them. If you are new to the event, say so. This is a great conversation starter. Regular attendees can introduce and welcome you to the event, or you will have common ground with other newbies. If the event includes food and drink, these are also conversational openings. We create social bonds over food. Be interested in the person you meet. Ask questions about them—their job, where they went to school, their hobbies, or their family. Most people are happy to talk about themselves when given the opportunity.

Bring a colleague. Bring someone with you to the event. You can converse with each other and invite others into your conversation. You can also introduce each other to new people. You can even make a game of it by taking turns doing so.

Take the initiative. Michelle's new job brought her to a new city. Once she had settled in, she joined a businesswomen's networking group. New in her workplace, she had no official role at these events, but she wanted to meet other like-minded women and begin building a social circle. Later her company decided to implement a community relations strategy, which included involving staff in community affairs, service clubs, and networking events. Naturally, Michelle was at the top of the list to represent the company.

Bonus Tip: Most of this advice applies to networking within the office as well!

FOLLOWING UP AFTER THE EVENT

If networking is successful, you will have collected business cards for relevant contacts. Follow-up is crucial, especially if you have promised information, further connection, or referrals. Integrity is important in relationship building, and a small promise is still a promise. In coaching, we say, "Be your word."

Social media follow-up. Using Facebook, Twitter, Instagram, and LinkedIn, we can network 24/7. There is no shortage of advice from Internet marketing gurus on how to grow friend and follower counts and increase connections. Most of this advice is misleading, and much of it borders on unethical. A general rule in building business or career connections online is to send connection requests only to people you've actually met in person. The same is true for accepting requests. Personally, I make exceptions if someone I trust refers the contact or we have many people or interests in common. You can connect on any social media platform, but the most professional online networking platform is LinkedIn. LinkedIn gives you the option to tap a Connect tab and send a generic request message. It's far better to personalize your message and provide context to the recipients, letting them know where you met them and why you are asking to connect. As with other business correspondence, keep it friendly and professional.

Bonus Tip: Before sending out any connection requests, be sure your social media profiles are up-to-date, including a current professional headshot.

E-mail follow-up. Include a reference to the event in the subject line of the e-mail follow-up. If someone has only met you for the first time, it is hard to recall where without context. Remember that you are connecting with other professionals whose inboxes are likely overflowing. Include a reference to something specific that you discussed or other information that identifies who you are in the body of the message. If you promised something specific—a referral, contact information, website link, or other information—include it in the message. Add an invitation for further contact, either digitally or in person.

MONITORING YOUR ONLINE BRAND AND PRESENCE

Are you aware of how you show up online? What is your online persona to someone who doesn't know you (or does)? Try this: Search for your first and last name on Google and see what comes up. You might be surprised. Carefully review the results. Check to see what is visible on your social media feeds in "public" mode. Are you completely comfortable with what you see there? If not, it's time to "weed your feed."

To be successful, we need to be authentic both online and offline. Therefore, it is difficult to separate the personal and the professional parts of our lives while remaining true to ourselves. It is good for our mental health to take a holistic approach to our lives and work, aiming for real alignment between who we are and what we do. The line is blurry, so it is important to know how much of our personal lives is visible to our coworkers, bosses, and professional contacts. Do you post about your workplace or your colleagues to friends on Facebook or Twitter? Think about the tone of these posts. Keep in mind that nothing in cyberspace is truly private. How would you feel if these posts were public?

Since the early days of social media, I've recommended that clients check the social media platforms of potential hires as part of their overall hiring process. It is not unusual for employers to delete applicants from the list as a result of these reviews. Think about your own posts. Now, imagine your current or future boss reading them. Better yet, imagine yourself in a leadership role. What do your posts say about you?

Negotiation

Without necessarily noticing it, most of us are practicing negotiation skills in our daily lives. We negotiate, often unconsciously, with our partners and families around meal plans and household chores, with friends around social activities or travel choices, with salespeople when purchasing our homes, cars, or household goods. The difference with negotiating in the workplace is that the stakes are often high. You may be negotiating on your own behalf for a raise, new position, or other perk or benefit or negotiating a deal on behalf of the company.

Skillful negotiation is an art form. It's a subtle give-and-take that is focused on an outcome that is beneficial to both parties. There is a tendency to enter negotiations looking for what we can get out of them rather than what we might have to give. Thoughtfully consider all sides of an issue. While you may be convinced that you deserve a raise, your boss or department head may not see it as clearly as you do. Ask yourself: What's in it for them?

HOW TO NEGOTIATE WELL

There are many scenarios in which you need good negotiation skills in the workplace. Perhaps you would like an increase in responsibility, a decrease in your workload, a new desk, a raise, or a different lunch schedule. Alternatively, your role may require you to negotiate with suppliers or other vendors on behalf of your workplace. You may need to close client deals or renegotiate contracts.

The more skilled you become at negotiating, the more successful you will be. There are three main facets to the negotiation process. These are preparation, process, and conclusion.

1. **Preparation.** Before entering the discussion, do your homework and research information relevant to your position. Clarify your goals and rationales. Give some thought to what is important to the other party.

2. **Process.** Agree on the process, set ground rules, and determine the schedule for the negotiation. Clarify your position and what it is you want. Offer rationales and listen carefully to the other party's concerns. Practice active listening and offer feedback to confirm mutual understanding. Agree on a process for next steps, should you not agree on an outcome. It might be difficult, but it is very useful to hold a collaborative and solution-oriented perspective during this phase. Be objective and willing to change positions if it is beneficial.

3. **Conclusion.** Whether there is an agreement or not, it is important to bring the negotiation to a close. Where there is agreement, be sure to record it in an appropriate way. If the negotiation is not going to result in the desired outcome, be prepared to walk away and go down gracefully. Unless the issue is very serious—a termination discussion, for example—there will be a tomorrow. You can agree to examine alternatives, revisit the issue after a set time period, or enter into a new process. Wherever possible, work to sustain the relationship.

Here are a few extra tips:

Consider the timing. Negotiating for a raise after the company has completed the yearly budget isn't going to work. When you're thinking about entering into a negotiation, think about the timing. What is the time frame that is most likely to lead to success?

Consider all sides. Most successful negotiations are ones where all parties feel that they have won. To see where the other party is coming from, ask them about their needs and concerns. If you can, address these. If you can't, be up front about it, and agree to get back to them with proposed solutions.

Practice active, engaged listening. Listen carefully to what you hear. Ask questions for clarity or to deepen your understanding of their position. Pay attention to body language and other nonverbal cues that might tell you how comfortable or uncomfortable the other party is with what you're proposing.

Self-manage. Stay calm and manage your emotions. Try not to be invested in the outcome, but rather follow the process and see where it leads. Many negotiations end in unexpected outcomes that are of benefit to both parties. Be open to that possibility.

ASSERTING YOURSELF

There are many situations in the workplace that do not require you to enter into formal negotiations in order to exert influence. Learning to assert yourself can go a long way in positioning you for success in the workplace. Assertive communication is neither passive nor aggressive. It is a direct form of communication marked by openness and respect.

Passive communicators tend to hold back their opinions and perspectives. Very often, people who are passive lack self-esteem, and look to keep the peace at any cost. Passive people often don't trust themselves and may not value their own thoughts or ideas. They often project nervousness, avoid eye contact, and fidget. Aggressive people tend to communicate through dominance, imposing their views on others and communicating with an air of superiority and disrespect. Their tone is often angry and their language hostile.

Assertive communicators are confident and clear and have few problems standing up for themselves in the workplace or otherwise. People who are assertive appear self-assured, positive, and poised. Assertive people can express their opinions while still validating the opinions of others. In the workplace there are several situations where assertiveness will pay off. Practicing assertiveness is important when speaking up at meetings, especially if you are offering an alternative or unpopular opinion. You may need to set boundaries at work with coworkers or with a boss or department head. You may want to influence decisions or persuade others to your point of view. Learning to take your own side is a life skill. Trusting yourself and knowing that you have a right to be heard and have an opinion will go a long way to helping you speak with confidence in any situation.

To assert yourself more effectively, try the following:

- Adjust your posture, breathe deeply, relax, and speak slowly.
- Make eye contact.

- Be sincere; show your enthusiasm, but do not exert undue pressure on others to agree.
- Express your preferences and priorities with *I* statements.
- Stick to factual descriptions rather than judging or assuming.
- Make clear, direct requests when you want something; avoid hinting or being indirect.
- Be respectful; do not belittle, personalize, or use sarcasm.
- Check your body language. Is your demeanor open and relaxed?
- Avoid getting emotional.
- When saying no, do so politely and firmly.
- If necessary, politely repeat your position and perspective until you feel heard.
- Use affirmative language and offer positive feedback in the exchange.

Write an Effective Proposal or Report

The quality of the proposals and reports you write can make or break your organization. You may be writing a proposal that will win a contract that brings in significant revenue, an application to a government agency on why it should approve a new project or product, or a report to charitable donors on how you have spent their money. At an internal level, you may be writing to your executive board or leadership team to report on the progress of an important assignment.

In any of these cases, your writing must be formally correct, clear, and accurate. However, in most cases, you don't want it to be dull. In general, your words will combine information with persuasion. This kind of writing should give the reader a clear set of messages on how your organization, your team, or your ideas are of benefit.

Here are some tips for increasing the effectiveness of a written proposal or report:

1. **Structure.** Begin by deciding on the structure of your report. What are the main headings, and what order should they follow? Make time for a short period of free writing or idea generation in which you can map out the key ideas you want to communicate and think about how they fit together. Consider the 5Ws and H as you develop your content. For either a report or proposal, start with a summary of what the reader can expect in the document.

2. **Visuals.** Many report writers find it useful to organize their thoughts in graphic form, using flow charts, overlapping circles, or matrices. Many readers will get more out of your report if you include one or more graphics.

3. **Start small.** Once you have your main headings organized—as well as your key messages and the key issues that you will address—feel free to write in short spurts. Go to a heading where you feel comfortable and write a summary of what you want to say. Then go to another heading and repeat the process. Start small and distribute your ideas to where they belong rather than trying to write from beginning to end.

4. **Include your audience.** Make use of web pages and reports that your audiences have published. If you are writing a proposal to a company, go to its website, cut out a sentence or two from the "About" page to show it that you know what it does. If you are writing to the board or leadership of your own organization, make use of its reports or past memos to demonstrate that your ideas align with its goals.

5. **Collaborate.** Leave adequate time in your work plan for review, approvals, and graphic design. Remember that good writing is collaborative. Have someone else proofread the draft. Ask someone to check your numbers. If the report requires approval from your superior or from a technical team, be ready to make structural changes or add supporting evidence. Finally, even if you don't have access to a professional graphic designer, it's important to ensure that your document has a clean-looking cover page, a consistent typography, and an open, readable feel.

CHOOSING THE CHANNEL: WHICH WAY TO SEND?

To decide on the proper channel, think through the content, format, and timeliness of your message. Note that company cultures vary. It is important to know and understand the expectations within your company or organization. If you work in government or the legal profession, there are specific regulatory parameters governing communication. Most workplaces have policies and protocols regarding external communication. Internally, you may be using platforms like Slack, Jira, Trello, Basecamp, or others to manage communication. You must adapt to the culture's expectations, not the other way around.

I use e-mail as a primary channel of business communication. It is not uncommon for clients and contacts to reach out on LinkedIn, Instagram, Facebook, or Twitter. Centennial and Millennial colleagues often send text or instant messages. To conduct business, however, I quickly move the communication to e-mail.

E-mail is more professional, it is easier to track and file correspondence and add attachments, and it is a platform that belongs to my business.

Here are some tips to help you decide how to choose the correct channel:

Content. Is the message purely professional, or does it have a social or personal component? Use e-mail with the appropriate CC, BCC, or Reply All etiquettes for purely professional messages, those that require input from a number of sources, or those that need oversight by a department head or organizational leadership. Save informal chat or text messages for social aspects of the workplace, such as coffee meetups, lunch dates, or office parties.

Format. Is the communication long or short form? It's best to circulate proposals, reports, agendas, meeting minutes, and other documents as attachments via e-mail. This is particularly true for any communication that forms a permanent record for the business.

Timeliness. If the communication requires immediate action or a delay will impact the productivity of the organization or business, convey it via e-mail with an appropriate subject line, by telephone, or in person. Consider IM or texting if the information is simple and straightforward or requires an immediate yes or no response. This also depends on the company culture around the use of chat or text messaging.

PART 2

Better Work Relationships

CHAPTER 5

AWARENESS OF SELF AND OTHERS

Self-awareness is inner work, but it is well worth embracing if you want to succeed in the workplace. In 2019, the American Management Association (AMA) reported on a study conducted by the organizational consulting firm Green Peak Partners. The study, titled "What Predicts Executive Success," found that a high self-awareness score was the strongest predictor of overall success for executives.

The study goes on to say that "an executive who is self-aware and good with staff will be better at working with clients and business partners, better at grasping and executing strategy, and better at delivering bottom-line results. These mostly lower-ego, trust-inspiring executives still hold the bar very high and demand strong performance but with a style that incorporates strong relational skills and respect."

The words *lower-ego* and *trust-inspiring* are the cornerstones for using awareness to build meaningful connections with colleagues, coworkers, and staff. Even if you're not an executive today, there is no doubt that if you are reading this book you are engaging in interpersonal relationships at work. If you hope to advance in your career, increasing your self-awareness by managing your ego and building trust will be critical.

Awareness allows us to tune in to what is happening in our inner dialogue as well as what is happening in the environment around us. This provides us with a higher level of social awareness as well as an emotional literacy whereby we can identify and process our own emotional states and empathize with others' emotional states. Crucial to effective communication in and out of the workplace, awareness of self and others is a core leadership quality.

Self-aware people have developed a sophisticated sense of their own emotional range, take responsibility for their actions and impact, are clear about boundaries, and can self-manage in difficult situations. This helps us tolerate workplace frustrations and navigate conflict, reduces stress, and makes us less impulsive and argumentative. As our awareness expands, we are able to put aside self-centeredness and see and understand others' perspectives. We become more naturally curious and open-minded. This leads to empathy, allowing us to see past differences and find common ground—which is more important than ever given the diverse, global nature of most workplaces.

Being Aware of Yourself

Sir John Whitmore, a founder of the contemporary executive coaching movement and author of *Coaching for Performance*, defines awareness as knowing what is happening around you and self-awareness as knowing what you are experiencing.

By heightening personal awareness, we can connect with sometimes hidden or unconscious aspects of ourselves that may be driving communication or decision-making processes without our conscious knowledge. We can discern the difference between reacting and responding. In a way, self-awareness is like simultaneously appearing in a movie and watching it. Our minds and bodies are engaged, our senses are taking in and interpreting our environment, and we are reacting and responding. At the same time, there is a somewhat detached observer self who is monitoring our behavior, a part that is "watching" the movie. A mentor of mine described this aspect of self as the part of us that knows we are sleeping when we are asleep. You can engage this observer self to heighten your awareness in interactions.

Many of us respond to situations, including key moments of decision-making at work, based on our social or family conditioning. We come into our careers armed with a set of preconceived ideas and expectations. Our responses, particularly to stress, confrontation, or conflict, are often automatic and reactive. The communication tools that may have been effective at home or at school may not serve as well in a professional setting. When we lack awareness, we lack choice. To quote Whitmore, "I am able to control only that of which I am aware. That of which I am unaware controls me. Awareness empowers me."

Here are some tips to increase your level of self-awareness:

Put the focus inside. Mindfulness is key to developing awareness. Take time each day to put your focus on your internal process. Slow your breathing and be aware of your physical sensations. What information are you getting proprioceptively (physically, from the outside environment) and processing internally? Acknowledge and name your thoughts and feelings.

Manage distractions. When engaging with someone in person, mute and put away your phone and step away from your screens. Allow yourself to focus fully on conscious, intentional interaction. Be aware of who and what you bring into your energy and emotional field. Managing distractions is also important to your mindfulness practice. Set aside time away from screens and devices to connect with yourself.

Be aware of your personas. Social media and the digital world have enabled us to develop personas, or versions of ourselves, that we use online. The persona you use in texting may not be the same as the persona you portray in a professional exchange or one that you use on a social media channel. Be aware of your personas and the different ways you interact. Having different personas can be fun, but it can also create dissonance. Can you align these personas to reflect who you truly are?

Consider your impact. Unless you are working completely remotely, your workplace is a shared environment. Be aware of the impact you have on others around you. Mute pings and notifications, keep your voice at a reasonable level when speaking out loud, and use earbuds or headphones if you are someone who needs to listen to music, podcasts, or the radio while working. In interpersonal interactions, notice how people respond to you. Are they drawn to you? Do they move away? Watch for verbal and nonverbal cues that reveal the impact you are having. A daily journal is a great tool to use to record what you notice.

Being Aware of Others

I started working with a bright and highly motivated young manager I'll call Javeed shortly after he was promoted to lead a small team of four. He struggled with the change in rank from coworker to manager regarding directing his former peers. Javeed also felt his boss was rejecting his ideas and perceived his boss as generally negative, leading to frustration and anger. He was having trouble controlling his emotions. He was stressed and irritated much of the time, and although he was not aware of it, he was taking out his frustration with short-temperedness and overly criticizing his team.

Through the coaching process, we established that Javeed needed to develop a greater awareness of his impact on others and of his emotional states and responses. Javeed was open to learning more about himself, willing to explore blind spots, and genuinely curious about how his emotions affected his ability to communicate and make decisions.

As part of the process, Javeed agreed to begin a daily journal. At the end of each workday, he took notes on his wins and challenges and reflected on his observations about himself and others, particularly in regard to interpersonal communication and emotional reactions. This practice enabled Javeed to look at himself and his workplace situations objectively. Over time he began to identify both positive and negative behavior patterns and their impact on others. He was also able to chart his growth and increasing capacity to deal with conflict. His openness to change and commitment to professional and personal growth helped him learn to identify his feelings, thoughts, and assumptions and to overcome blind spots. You can do this, too.

Step outside yourself. Focus your attention outside yourself. Pause for a few minutes each day and observe the people around you. Pay attention to what you see and hear. What do you feel or sense in the environment? Be mindful of your coworkers. What is their body language, tone, or stress level? Practicing daily mindfulness will help you attune to what is around you and increase your awareness of others. Use a journal to track your observations.

Practice listening first. The next time you step into a meeting or the lunchroom, rather than launching right into the discussion, practice attentive listening. What is the emotional tone of casual conversation? Who is being heard? What nuances are you aware of? How might these cues and nuances inform the way you communicate in this setting? Use your awareness of others to assess the best communications approach.

Practice awareness online. It is more difficult to do, but you can demonstrate your awareness (or expose your lack of it) online as well. I recently sent a text to a colleague expressing frustration and worry about a large project. She texted back: "I hear you. Let's book a call." A similar e-mail to another colleague received this response: "At least you've got a large project to work on!" I'm sure it is easy for you to discern which colleague is more aware.

Bonus Tip: A great way to develop awareness is to watch a video of people interacting with the audio turned off. Take notes of your interpretation of the feelings indicated by the cues and signals you see. Then watch it again with sound. See how accurately you interpreted the interaction.

Best Practices for Better Awareness

Adopt a mindfulness practice. Consider meditation training or classes or use one of the many mindfulness or meditation apps available for smartphones. Take time each day to simply be present to yourself and your surroundings and attune to your senses.

Become an observer. Practice noticing the way you react in different situations. Consciously take the observer seat and see if you can identify your thoughts, feelings, strengths, and weaknesses in different interactions. Track your insights by keeping a daily journal either online or in a notebook.

Seek feedback from others. We all have blind spots. Ask a handful of trusted friends or colleagues to list what they perceive as your strengths and weaknesses and provide constructive feedback to you in areas where you may not yet be self-aware.

Manage screens and devices. When with others, focus. Mute devices, step away from screens, and seek opportunities to engage face-to-face, either in person or via video chat. Engage in co-present conversations.

Consider your impact. Every workplace has a beautiful diversity of personalities, styles, and approaches. Consider the impact that yours might have on others in your workplace including those of different cultural or social backgrounds. Be sensitive and practice empathy.

CHAPTER 6

EMPATHY

The term *empathy* comes from the Greek *empatheia*, meaning "feeling into." Empathy is the ability to put yourself in another person's shoes and perceive their subjective experience. We experience empathy when we sense or feel another's emotional state or when we can take their perspective, identifying and understanding another's feelings in a given situation.

People often confuse empathy with sympathy. Empathy is the ability to understand and share another's feelings, while sympathy involves feeling sorry for or pitying another. While you may feel sympathy toward flood victims, for example, you may not have true empathy for them unless you have experienced something similar yourself.

Developing empathy requires us to make a deep connection with our own emotional states and to become comfortable in the emotional field. Many people are uncomfortable with displays of emotion, particularly those feelings that we perceive as negative such as sorrow, anger, jealousy, or fear. Often, the first impulse when faced with these emotions in ourselves or others is to avoid them.

In the personal development workshops I lead, participants can experience a profound connection with themselves or resonate deeply with others in the room as we explore questions of meaning, belonging, and personal legacy. Tears are not uncommon. It is interesting to observe other participants' reactions. Some sit calmly, tears in their own eyes, while others fidget or begin immediately passing tissues. It takes a high level of self-awareness and acceptance to hold another's emotional field. While we are naturally moved to comfort one another, often our well-meaning pats on the shoulder and tissue passing are attempts to avoid our own discomfort and distract others from their feelings. Highly self-aware people can attune to others' feelings, express empathy, and hold the space for emotional process.

Why does this matter in the workplace? According to the *Harvard Business Review*, empathy is "a deep emotional intelligence that is closely connected to cultural competence. Empathy enables those who possess it to see the world through others' eyes and understand their unique perspectives." Empathy connects us to one another, creating resonance and helping people feel seen, heard, and understood. When people feel heard and understood, they feel safe and become more receptive to other viewpoints, collaborative problem-solving, and risk-taking. This fosters an environment of trust that creates bonds, strengthens relationships, and builds loyalty. In this kind of environment, people feel safe to express their ideas and opinions, creating a crucible in which companies can grow, innovate, and thrive.

Considering Others' Feelings

One of the key challenges in considering others' feelings is that usually we are operating in the dark in that we can only assume we know what they are experiencing. We hear what people say, read nonverbal cues, interpret their meaning and then make assumptions based on our observations. The problem is we often mistake our assumptions for truth. We then formulate our responses and reactions or justify our positions based on these interpretations. Despite considerable differences in upbringing, experience, personalities, cultural backgrounds, and communication styles, we assume we *know* how other people feel.

My friend and mentor, Drucilla Desabrais, founder of the *Adventures in Living* personal development series, introduced me to a highly effective communication model many years ago. Based on the work of Bennett Wong and Jock McKeen of the Haven Institute, the model is designed to help validate our assumptions and interpretations by checking things out as we engage in the communication process.

Wong and McKeen put it this way: "By learning to check out our interpretations—without getting caught up in arguments about who's 'right' and who's 'wrong'—we take a huge step in understanding and expressing ourselves and expanding our worlds to include others' realities. We will also be better able to accept and express our thoughts and feelings—and understand those of others—without letting these dictate how we live. We will be able to formulate our intentions more clearly and take actions that are congruent, self-responsible, and sensitive to others." The model describes what goes on when people try to communicate and is based on the following:

Perception. Perception is based on inputs we take in through our five senses. Communication based on perception starts with sensory input. For example, "When I see, hear, taste, smell, touch . . . "

Interpretation. We marry what we perceive with context—what we know about one another and the circumstances as well as our own background and experience—and we attribute meaning to what we perceive. This is our interpretation and would be framed this way: "I believe, think, imagine, judge, speculate . . . " It does not start with "I feel . . . " Feelings develop based on proprioceptive input (perception) and interpretation.

Check it out. At this stage of the communication you may want to check out your interpretation to see if it is accurate. The model is organic, so you may prefer to share your feelings and then check out and validate your perceptions and interpretation. Either way, what is important is that you check out your assumptions with the other person.

Feelings. Feelings are either positive, negative, or ambiguous. They are distinct from our thoughts and induce us to move either toward (make a connection) or away from (reject) one another. Share your feelings based on the information you receive.

Intention. Be clear about your intention. What was the purpose of the communication, and what do you intend to do?

Action. What you do as a result of the exchange that is congruent with the information you receive and sensitive to the other person's actual state.

In this model, nobody is ever right or wrong. You can only agree or disagree. Intentionally taking this view allows space for dialogue rather than position-taking. It is an approach based in awareness and consciously choosing to forsake rigid stances in favor of open communication. In coaching, we have a similar viewpoint that holds that "everybody is right, only partially." This is a positive frame that helps shift perspective from the "I am right, you are wrong" paradigm that governs much of our communication.

Imagine this scenario: Michelle noticed that Greta's eyes were red. Michelle knows that management transferred a project from Greta to another coworker earlier that day and assumes Greta is upset about this. Michelle said, "I see that your eyes are red. I think you must be upset about the project allocation, and I feel drawn to support you if I can. First, let me check. Are you upset about the project allocation? Is there anything I can do?" Greta laughed. "No, I'm not upset at all. I have hay fever, and it's really acting up. Actually, I'm relieved that the project has moved off my desk."

Michelle was operating on assumptions based on the context that she had about the workflow as well as projecting feelings she might have had if management had pulled the task from her own desk. By checking it out, she learned more about Greta—that she succumbs to hay fever and she has a full workload. Greta learned that Michelle was there to support her if needed.

We can capture the heart of this model this way: Ask, listen, share, and **check it out** with the other person.

Considering Others' Backgrounds

Glassdoor is one of the top international job recruitment and placement agencies in the world. It conducted a study in which 67% of job seekers claimed that diversity in the workplace is important to them. Further, Glassdoor reviewed research from Harvard, McKinsey, Gallup, and peer-reviewed studies and found that diverse teams produce financial returns 33% higher than industry norms and that gender diversity alone could grow the U.S. economy by more than 5%. *Diversity Matters*, the McKinsey report, states, "More diverse companies are better able to win top talent and improve their customer orientation, employee satisfaction, and decision-making, and all that leads to a virtuous cycle of increasing returns. This in turn suggests that other kinds of diversity—for example, in age, sexual orientation, and experience (such as a global mind-set and cultural fluency)—are also likely to bring some level of competitive advantage for companies that can attract and retain such diverse talent."

Numerous studies conclude not only that diversity is good for the bottom line but also that the representation of different populations in ethnicity, race, ability, language, nationality, age, socioeconomic status, gender, sexual orientation, or religion contributes to increased productivity, better performance, and improved idea generation, decision-making, and problem-solving. In today's workplace the affordances of technology enable us to deal with clients, customers, and colleagues from around the world. Working in a global and culturally diverse context means we must develop what the McKinsey report refers to as "cultural fluency": learning to discern context and develop understanding despite language barriers; differing etiquettes, protocols, and social norms; and lack of direct personal experience of a culture or status.

Remember Javeed? He was in a budget meeting with his boss, Paul, when he received a text from his wife notifying him that his mother had fallen ill. Javeed quickly gathered his belongings and left the meeting, saying only, "I must go." The next day, Javeed was called into Paul's office to face an angry boss. Paul loudly expressed his disappointment that Javeed had left the meeting abruptly, without explanation, particularly with a budget deadline looming.

Based on his background, it was natural for Javeed to drop everything and return home when he heard that his mother was sick. He comes from a culture that puts family ahead of everything, including work. In his culture, personal and professional life are kept separate, and Javeed is not comfortable discussing his personal life with his coworkers. Javeed struggled to explain his priorities to Paul.

During the interaction, Paul noticed Javeed's discomfort. Setting aside his own anger, he instead adopted an attitude of curiosity. "Javeed," he said, "I genuinely don't understand your choice to leave the meeting. Please help me." This approach created space for Javeed to share not only the cultural expectations related to family, but also his often-overwhelming feelings of responsibility toward the extended family members who shared his roof. As someone responsible for the welfare of others in his role, Paul genuinely empathized, saying, "I know the feeling." The interaction was an important one as it helped Paul understand Javeed's cultural context and revealed shared common ground.

Paul was genuinely angry Javeed had left the meeting without explanation, but he suspected that cultural differences were at play. Practicing self-awareness, Paul paid attention to his internal dialogue, reserved judgment, and asked questions. This is the way to build bridges and open the door for deeper communication and mutual learning.

HOW TO RESPECT CULTURAL DIFFERENCES

Keep communication simple and polite. In chapter 2, we covered the importance of simplicity and clarity in effective communication. This becomes even more essential where there are cultural or language differences. When communicating with someone from another culture, mind your manners and avoid using slang words and phrases. If you are presenting or reporting, incorporate visuals where possible.

Learn about differences. Learn about different cultural backgrounds either by asking your coworkers polite questions or through study. Take a cultural sensitivity course or request one at your workplace. Consider studying a language or specific culture or hosting a lunch and learn where colleagues exchange information about their backgrounds.

Be aware of bias. It is easy to see the world through our own or the predominant cultural lens. Bias is often unconscious, but by practicing self-awareness, we can begin to recognize it. Become sensitive to different religious observances or cultural celebrations and customs. Keep in mind that abstinence from certain foods or alcohol or specific modes of dress can reflect cultural norms.

Practice empathy. Beyond our distinct cultural or social backgrounds, we are all human and share some level of common experience. Try to find common ground and to empathize with situations where you can relate. The *Harvard Business Review* study mentioned earlier in this chapter reveals that "empathetic understanding is indispensable in increasingly diverse markets . . . and in other cultures around the world. Neither technical knowledge nor business acumen suffices. You must be sincerely interested in understanding other cultural preferences and choices."

Learn to appreciate, acknowledge, and celebrate differences. Remember that diversity, and sensitivity to it, is a strength in the workplace.

HOW'S YOUR TONE?

Tone, something we convey easily in spoken communications, becomes tricky when it comes to professional written communication, particularly in the digital environment. Tone conveys the attitude of the message (and sender/writer) and provides important signals as to how the receiver is meant to feel receiving it. Think back to the example of the e-mail correspondence between Carole and Devin in chapter 3. Carole's message was confusing as her light and casual tone belied the actual urgency of her message. Devin's one-word response, with its complete absence of tone, implied disrespect. Consider the difference in tone in these three sentences:

1. "I suggest we continue with the project as outlined."

2. "Continue with the project as outlined."

3. "Continue with the project as outlined, please."

What tone do you infer from each? To a large degree, the way you interpret tone will depend on your experience with the sender. Sentence 1 implies that there is some room for questioning, while sentence 2 is a directive. Despite including a polite *please* at the end, sentence 3 could be construed as sarcastic depending on your relationship with the sender or the circumstances surrounding the project. Context is always important. In short-form communication, providing detailed context can be difficult. Always check your correspondence for tone and be aware of the feelings it may elicit in the person receiving it.

Best Practices for Greater Empathy

Put yourself in the others' shoes. Even if you have no direct experience of their situation, try to imagine yourself in their position and consciously take their perspective.

Practice nonjudgment. Notice when your thoughts take a judgmental turn. Try to put your judgment aside and stay open.

Explore your own emotional range. Take note of your relative comfort or discomfort with emotional expression and begin naming and identifying what you are feeling. Remember that thoughts and feelings are different.

Be fully present and listen actively. Put away your smartphone. Practice self-awareness and attune to your inner dialogue and proprioceptive responses.

Take opportunities to "step outside yourself." Try to look at situations and interactions objectively and learn to read the room. Adopt regular mindfulness practices such as simple meditation or journaling to help build muscle in this area.

Be aware of and sensitive to cultural and social differences.
Cultivate an attitude of curiosity and respect for others. Become
genuinely interested in learning about differences and identifying
how differences add strength and bring value to decision-making,
problem-solving, and productivity.

Communicate. Share what you are sensing and feeling and offer
simple, judgment-free responses such as "I hear you," "I understand," or "Tell me more."

Avoid assumption. Trust your intuition, but don't assume
certainty. If you sense that something is troubling a coworker or
that you have misinterpreted their meaning or intent, check it
out. This is the only way to validate your interpretation.

CHAPTER 7

CONNECTING WITH OTHERS

Abraham Maslow's theory on the hierarchy of needs suggests that a basic set of human needs motivates people. Researchers usually show Maslow's hierarchy as a pyramid, with the most basic physiological needs such as food, water, sex, and sleep forming the base of the pyramid. Once we meet these foundational needs, we are motivated to secure them and ensure our safety and the safety of our families, seeking shelter, employment, and ongoing health. We then move up the hierarchy to fulfill our basic needs for love and belonging, self-esteem, and the esteem of others and then further to self-actualization, finding purpose and meaning in our lives.

Through work we are seeking to fulfill our most basic security needs as well as our higher needs for fulfillment. Squarely in the middle of these are our needs for belonging, affection, recognition, and respect. In my coaching practice, one of the most common issues clients bring to their sessions is what I call "the longing for belonging." They are deeply aware of the need to connect, first and foremost to themselves—to recognize their deep personal needs, desires, and motivations—and then to find like-minded people—friends, allies, and colleagues who can love and accept them and champion their goals and growth.

Common Internet wisdom suggests that on average Americans spend nearly one-third of their adult life at work—more than 90,000 hours over a lifetime! Given that humans are driven to meet a common set of fundamental needs, it is only natural that we hope and expect to have these needs met, at least to some degree, in the workplace. To truly feel loved, accepted, and respected, we must connect in an authentic way with other human beings. If you think of your workplace as a community, there are several ways to foster a sense of connection among colleagues.

Be inclusive. Create opportunities to include others in committees, social activities, and events. Don't neglect remote colleagues.

Practice deep democracy. Deep democracy is a process work framework, developed by psychologist Arny Mindell. It suggests that all voices and opinions matter, even the unpopular ones. Value diverse opinions and acknowledge risk-taking.

Share goals, values, and purpose. Connection is not only about other people, it is also about shared purpose, values, and goals. Be transparent with colleagues and coworkers about what motivates you, what you value, and why. Explore their values. Find common ground.

Foundations of Connection

As humans, we connect on several different levels—physical, emotional, intellectual, and spiritual. Traditionally, the workplace has been a physical space where we engage intellectually with our colleagues and coworkers. Today, much work takes place remotely, via devices and screens. Unless work is physical in its nature, such as in the construction trades, health care, or professional sports, actual physical connection is limited to handshakes, a high-five or pat on the back, or a reassuring tap on the arm or shoulder. Most other physical contact in the workplace is discouraged, given the risks of people misinterpreting touch.

For much of the twentieth century, the emotional and spiritual dimensions of human connection did not factor into the workplace equation. In 1995, Daniel Goleman wrote a groundbreaking book called *Emotional Intelligence—Why It Can Matter More Than IQ* (Bantam, 1995), which redefined the role factors such as self-awareness, self-discipline, and empathy play in success. Society has widely accepted that healthy workplaces are ones where emotional intelligence is high and employees are engaged on all levels.

Your workplace may or may not have structures such as cross-departmental meetings, an explicit mission or set of values, or processes for inclusive decision-making. While these organizational systems do help support and build connection, there is much you can do as an individual to increase connection at work. Obviously effective communication, the subject of this book, is central to establishing connection. As we explored in part 1, there is much more to communication than simply transmitting messages back and forth.

Clear, simple, direct, and succinct communication will ensure transmission of your messages, but the effect and impact of the exchange are what determine the quality of the relationships you build. At heart, good communication is about establishing connection. Foundational to establishing good connection are trust-building characteristics like integrity, mutual respect, curiosity, open-mindedness, humility, and a willingness to be vulnerable with others. Developing your skill in the areas of collaboration, cooperation, active listening, and self-awareness will all contribute to creating and maintaining connections.

Connection is not just about meeting our personal needs for belonging and friendship. In its research into bridging the engagement gap, Jostle, an intranet development company, found that "the more people connect and relate to one another as peers, the more they understand how the organization fits together. This is especially true of teams that work in different locations, in different time zones, and with different skills." Connecting with others connects you to the bigger organizational picture. As you sustain and grow these connections, both formally and informally, you will be developing a trusted network of professional support across your workplace.

RESPECT

Respectful workplaces are ones where people feel valued, trusted, and encouraged to fully participate and engage. They are free of bullying and harassment, diversity is welcomed, and interactions are positive. Not all workplaces fit this bill. Developing a culture of respect is an ongoing process and one that requires the conscious engagement of everyone. Respect means treating people the way you wish to be treated. The foundation of respect is a belief that other people have the right to be treated with dignity and that their rights, opinions, and experience matter. You can demonstrate respect in the workplace in the following ways:

- Treat everyone with courtesy and kindness. Be polite in your interactions.

- Seek out the opinions and ideas of others and attribute credit where credit is due.

- Practice good listening skills by giving your attention to others first before expressing your own ideas and avoid interrupting while they speak.

- Acknowledge the contributions of others. Offer corrective feedback in private and praise in public.

- Avoid nitpicking. Everyone makes mistakes. Learn to tolerate imperfection (your own and others').

- Never name-call, insult, belittle, demean, or patronize a coworker or their ideas. These behaviors are the opposite of respect and over time can constitute bullying.

- Be inclusive and invite coworkers to participate in meetings, events, committees, volunteer opportunities, and social outings as appropriate. Do not marginalize or leave people out.

- Be aware of tone of voice, body language, and your overall demeanor in interactions.

HUMILITY

The essence of humility is truth. It involves taking a fearless look at ourselves and facing the truth of what we find—our strengths, weaknesses, blind spots, insecurities, and mistakes. To demonstrate humility, you must become uncomfortably honest about your failings. This doesn't mean you need to dwell in the negative, have a low opinion of yourself, or beat yourself up (as self-help jargon often describes it). However, it does mean being willing to see yourself as human and, as such, flawed.

Many of us have been conditioned to believe that strength and humility cannot coexist and to see humility as weak. New insights and perspectives are challenging that conditioning, suggesting that characteristics such as humility and vulnerability are indicators of courage and are strengths in and of themselves.

We are also coming to accept that there is a duality to being human whereby we can be brave and fearful simultaneously or humble and self-confident or competent and uncertain. People who can admit to their mistakes, ask questions when they are doubtful, and embrace the notion of duality are more apt to make strong connections in the workplace, be respected for their approach, and make good leaders. According to the *Journal of Management Studies*, researchers have well documented the effectiveness of leader humility as a competency.

Reflect on your own experiences. Can you think of a time when coworkers admitted a mistake or asked good questions when they weren't sure about how to proceed on something? What impression did that make? Did you dismiss them as incompetent or weak, or did you admire their courage and see how their approach made for a better outcome?

According to Bill Benjamin, a trainer for the Institute for Health and Human Potential, these are the key behaviors that comprise the humility competency:

- Admit when you are wrong, say "I am sorry," and take responsibility for your actions.
- Laugh at yourself occasionally and don't take yourself too seriously.
- Openly and graciously share the learnings acquired from your failings and hard experiences.
- Readily admit when you are overwhelmed and ask for help.
- Willingly choose ideas other than your own, say "thank you" and openly give credit for work.
- Listen without jumping to conclusions.

VULNERABILITY

Much credit goes to research professor and author Brene Brown, whose 2010 TEDxHouston talk "The Power of Vulnerability" went viral and opened a worldwide conversation on vulnerability and honesty. In her book *Daring Greatly: How the Courage to Be Vulnerable Transforms the Way We Live, Love, Parent, and Lead* (Avery, 2015), Brown says, "Vulnerability is the core, the heart, the center, of meaningful human experiences." She further defines vulnerability as "uncertainty, risk, and emotional exposure."

This sounds a little scary, right? After all, why would we want to open ourselves to uncertainty, risk, and emotional exposure at work? As we've discussed in this chapter, a fundamental human need is the need for connection, and the only way we can truly connect with each other is if we risk vulnerability. It takes courage to be vulnerable, and that courage will allow you to have difficult conversations, stand up for your beliefs, and admit mistakes. Developing a degree of comfort with uncertainty and risk is a good indicator of your ability to be creative and innovative. It means you'll be able to try new things and increases your capacity to encourage others to do the same. Your vulnerability will help create a more courageous culture where coworkers can trust one another and risk the uncomfortable conversations that are so important to growth—both personal and professional.

Finding Common Ground

Beyond establishing connection, building empathy, and helping overcome cultural or social differences, finding common ground is key to doing our best work. Unless you are a team of one, you rely on others in your workplace to collaborate and cooperate on projects large and small. Finding the common ground with coworkers either personally or professionally will help create an environment conducive to effective teamwork and mutual success.

We use the phrase "finding common ground" because it is something we must seek. Our commonalties are often not as clear to us as our differences. This requires effort, patience, and respect for others. We must focus on areas of agreement rather than areas of disagreement. We must be aware of power imbalances, differences in skill level or aptitude, or access to information and try to mitigate inequities.

When trying to find common ground personally or professionally, here are a few tactics you can employ:

Focus on the big picture. What are you trying to achieve in the long run? What do you each agree defines success? Find agreement and then bring the focus of your interactions to the desired outcome.

Anticipate challenges. What barriers might you encounter as you try to establish common ground and achieve your goals? List these and discuss tactics for dealing with them.

Practice intentionality. Identify the purpose of achieving the common ground. What is it you both (all) hope to gain? How will things change as a result?

Be curious. If there's something you don't understand or a proposed solution you can't see, investigate! Ask questions to seek clarity and be willing to have your perspective changed. Try to learn more about others' opinions or the options they are proposing.

Eliminate either/or thinking. Try taking a "Yes, and . . . " position rather than a "No, but . . . " stance. This validates the ideas and opinions of others and enhances the ideas rather than dismissing them. Remember, "Everybody is right, only partially."

Bonus Tip: Are you familiar with the Venn diagram? It is a picture of two overlapping circles. The overlap is common ground; the other areas are differences and disagreements. Draw this with your team and discuss the overlap. You can also do this privately if you are exploring differences and trying to find common ground in interpersonal issues.

Ownership, Accountability, and Apologizing

Taking ownership and having personal accountability are two cornerstones of what I call uber-maturity (which has nothing to do with the popular ride-hailing service; I am using it as we do the word *super* in English). Uber-maturity requires us to take 100% responsibility for our experiences. Certainly, there are circumstances over which we have no control, but we are completely in control of how we respond to those circumstances. As adults, we can find the meaning, purpose, and relevance of any situation based on our own set of guideposts. Self-responsibility is one of the most powerful assets you can develop, one that ultimately frees you from perceiving yourself or anyone else as a victim of circumstances.

Even though Javeed, in the example in the previous chapter, was frustrated and unhappy about the perceived rejections from his boss, he took ownership of the situation and sought solutions that did not involve his boss having to change. He investigated his preconceived notions about how he expected his boss to react. He realized that he was interpreting valid questions his boss asked as rejection. He revised his approach strategy and began using the communication model that we described in chapter 6. He checked out his interpretations and discovered that his boss was willing to explore new ideas if his questions could be answered. Even if the dialogue had gone another way, with Javeed finding that his boss was not open to new ideas, that information would be useful. Javeed could stop wasting his time, energy, and anger on a situation over which he had no control.

When Javeed realized that he was taking out his frustrations on his team with his short temper and criticism, he apologized to them collectively and individually. He owned his lack of self-awareness about the impact his emotions were having on his coworkers and collaborated with them on strategies for change. As you can imagine, this was a very vulnerable moment for Javeed. Interestingly, during the exchange, one of his team members revealed that she, too, had an anger management problem and was concerned about how it might be impacting the team at work. Javeed was able to express empathy and had developed the skill and confidence to coach her forward.

Apologizing effectively is not easy. It requires us to take full ownership of our actions and to approach the interaction with humility and sincere intention. Knowing when to apologize can also be tricky. A good rule of thumb is if you suspect that something you did, either by accident or on purpose, hurt someone's feelings or negatively impacted or interfered with their work, apologize and clean it up.

Here are a few tips for effective apologies:

Acknowledge. Articulate the wrongdoing or mistake. Be specific and clear about the matter about which you are apologizing.

Accept responsibility. Take ownership of your actions and their impact. Don't equivocate with explanations or rationalizations. Avoid saying "but."

Apologize. Say you are sorry out loud (or in writing if a face-to-face apology is not possible). Be sincere.

Offer amends. State your intention for change, amends, or redress, and then take the promised action. Not every apology will be effective, but if you have made a sincere effort and taken responsibility for your part, you can move on peacefully and with integrity.

Best Practices for Better Connection

Practice empathy. Be willing to take the perspective of others and identify with their thoughts and feelings. Communicate your understanding and awareness.

Model respect. Be respectful of the thoughts and ideas of others and treat people the way you would like to be treated.

Ask questions. Become curious about the opinions, point of view, and perspectives of your coworkers and colleagues. Seek understanding and clarity around social or cultural differences.

Act with integrity. Be your word and follow through on promises. The adage "actions speak louder than words" is especially true when building trust.

Take ownership. If you've made a mistake, say so, and take responsibility for the outcome. Apologize if you are in the wrong and make amends or offer redress if possible. Remember that you are 100% responsible for your experiences.

Seek common ground. Look for commonalities rather than differences, particularly when the stakes are high or uncertainty prevails.

Be open to personal growth. Expand your self-awareness. Practice mindfulness and seek opportunities for self-discovery. Everyone has blind spots. Be open to getting feedback about yours and willing to acknowledge your strengths and weaknesses and adjust for them.

Acknowledge others. Validate the experience and success of others, both publicly and privately. Catch your colleagues and coworkers doing things right!

CHAPTER 8

THE IMPORTANCE OF LISTENING WELL

You are likely familiar with the old saying "There's a reason you have two ears and one mouth." It implies that listening is twice as important as speaking. Listening also has two components. While hearing is an automatic, involuntary brain response to sound, listening is focused and intentional. Good listening is active, requiring a decision on our part to pay attention to what is said rather than passively hearing what is said. Listening well requires a commitment on our part to be self-aware, minimize internal dialogue and distractions, and engage with the speaker to validate our understanding of what they are trying to communicate. The goal of effective communication is *mutual* understanding. Good listening is not simply perceiving the facts and knowledge that one is conveying but understanding the information *from the speaker's point of view*.

Most contemporary workplaces are fast-moving environments where priorities, initiatives, and strategies are constantly changing. Knowledge and information transfer at dizzying speeds via a range of communication channels. Colleagues, coworkers, clients, and managers with vastly different life experiences, cultural biases, and communication styles deliver messages either effectively or ineffectively. In such environments, developing good listening skills is critical to ensuring accurate and timely information-sharing. The ability to listen well means that you can understand and act on information that is critical to good decision-making, building workplace trust and connection, and reducing potential conflict. Listening skills are key to effective communication.

Are You Really Listening?

In chapter 6, we covered the role of self-awareness and empathy in effective communication. As you become more self-aware, you will notice the impact it has on your ability to listen well. Self-aware listeners can identify their filters, understanding that they have biases toward hearing certain things and not others. There is a common tendency to filter out negative, critical, or unpleasant information (or conversely to focus on those things and filter out compliments). When you are really listening well to another person, you can restrain yourself from interrupting, diverting the conversation to another topic, or debating the merits of another's position while it is still being described. Good listeners avoid leaping into the conversation with advice before one asks for it or solving problems before they fully understand them. While empathy is an important quality in building connection and relating to others, good listeners are mindful that overly identifying—referring everything that is said back to our own experience—can interfere with fully grasping another's point of view. Effective listeners are more focused on really hearing what the other person is saying than in expressing their own opinion, perspective, or experience.

Do you remember the strategy we discussed for Nala back in chapter 2? She was having trouble influencing her new management peers, overcommunicating, and failing to adapt her style to their needs. The solution for her was to begin breaking her ideas down into smaller chunks, presenting them conceptually, and then *listening carefully* to the feedback she received. This strategy certainly had to do with how she verbalized her ideas, but a significant factor in her success was her ability, through practice, to listen to the feedback she was receiving. Nala needed to truly listen and comprehend the point of view of her peers without placating them with false assurances of her understanding. Through listening well, Nala was able to understand their concerns and tailor her message to their needs.

Skillful listeners engage with the speaker, offering genuine interest and curiosity about not only the subject matter, but also the speaker's perspectives, feelings, opinions, and insights. Over time and with practice, you will be able to identify your strengths and weaknesses as a listener and improve your listening skills.

Qualities of an Effective Listener

Do you know whether you are a good listener? Think about someone you know—a close friend, or a trusted coworker, someone you reach out to when you need to express your thoughts or are puzzling through a problem. Chances are you reach out to these people because they are good listeners. It is likely that they possess the following characteristics:

- They pay attention to you and what you are saying.
- They look you in the eye and give you nonverbal cues that demonstrate interest—nodding or smiling appropriately.
- They don't interrupt, letting you finish your thoughts before offering their feedback or opinion.
- They repeat back what they are hearing in their own words, checking out their interpretation. For example, a good listener might say, "Are you saying . . . ?" or "Do you mean . . . ?"
- When you are finished speaking, they ask questions for clarification or open-ended questions to expand the conversation further.

Now think about a recent conversation you've had where someone was trying to convey something relatively important to you. Did you pay attention and offer nonverbal indications not only that you were listening, but also that you had heard their meaning? Did you ask clarifying or open-ended questions to encourage even greater understanding?

A good listener does more than simply hear the words. A good listener strives to understand the meaning the speaker hopes to communicate. Further, a good listener offers empathy and encourages the speaker to verbalize comfortably what they wish to articulate. This kind of listening builds trust.

In the digital age, attention is currency. Offering someone our undivided attention not only helps ensure effective communication, it also conveys that we value the person and our relationship with them. We are showing these individuals that they matter and that their ideas and opinions also matter.

The online communications environment poses special challenges when it comes to listening. The most significant issue is the medium's binary nature. The communication is taking place in two separate and distinct parts, without the benefit of auditory cues such as tone and inflection and without the visual cues that can impart meaning. Because the communication takes place on devices, we are left without the free flow of face-to-face human interaction.

Online video communication tools such as FaceTime, Skype, and Zoom offer us the advantage of face-to-face engagement but can be subject to poor technical quality, multiple interruptions, and background noise. E-mails, instant messages, and social media posts are one-way communication tools. What many people don't realize is that reading messages, while visual, requires auditory processing. Essentially, we "hear" what we see when we read. In this context, good listening and the ability to process and understand what we've read become even more important.

Here is an example of a situation that demonstrates the importance of good listening skills. You met Devin earlier in the book. He works in the communications department of a large, complex organization. He hopes to eventually progress through the department into a leadership role. He is part of a relatively new team that cowrites, edits, and distributes the corporate newsletter both in print and online. In a meeting, his boss, Kim, raised a couple of concerns about a recent issue of the newsletter. Devin reacted defensively, interrupting his boss to explain his point of view before they fully identified the problems. His colleague, Michelle, waited until Kim described and discussed the problems and then asked clarifying questions to be sure she understood what they needed to fix. Michelle followed up the meeting with an e-mail confirming her understanding of the next steps.

As the leader of the department, Kim continually has her eyes open for up-and-coming talent as she looks to fill and expand key roles. "In meetings," says Kim, "I pay attention to who is listening carefully and asking the right questions rather than to who has the right answers. In a fast-paced organization, clarity is everything." Today, Michelle is on track to take over department leadership.

Good listening requires us not only to be able to read cues, ask meaningful questions, and understand intent. It also requires us to suspend our own inferences, judgments, and assumptions. In a professional setting we must also manage our emotional reactions, fears, and insecurities. We'll talk more about this in the next section.

Common Listening Blocks

Much like writing well, listening well requires focus and concentration. There are many obstacles that can stand in the way of good listening. Naturally, environment is a factor. There can be actual physical impediments to hearing well such as background noise, other concurrent conversations, and digital distractions such as flashing screens, pop-ups, or audible notifications and alerts. If your conversation is taking place in a hearing conducive environment and you have managed the external distractions, our biggest listening block is that we are typically attuned to our own inner dialogue rather than focused on what the other person is saying.

Our inner dialogue is composed of a constellation of thoughts that include comparing, judging, dreaming, anticipating, and rehearsing. We may appear to be listening—we are quiet, looking attentively at the speaker, perhaps nodding our heads, but our minds are busy elsewhere. We are only pseudo-listening, feigning interest while involved in our own thoughts and feelings. Let's examine some of the ways these tendencies hijack our ability to truly listen.

Comparing. Assessing who is smarter, brighter, or better and reflecting on your own (better/worse) viewpoint, opinion, or situation while the other person is communicating theirs. Comparing is often rooted in a lack of self-esteem, or fear of others viewing you as "less than."

Judging. Negatively evaluating and drawing conclusions based on personal bias or preconceived ideas and "writing off" the message before you fully comprehend it. A close cousin to judging is becoming triggered, where something that is said provokes a fearful, hostile, or defensive reaction in you. You mentally withdraw or begin formulating your "attack" or defense rather than hearing the other out.

Dreaming. Something that is said reminds you of something else in your experience, and you enter a strange, dreamlike world . . . appearing to listen but actually engaged in making a shopping list, recalling your childhood, or thinking about what you're going to have for lunch. Daydreaming can also occur as a kind of mental "checking out" or escape hatch if the conversation is sensitive or uncomfortable. Be aware if this happens for you.

Anticipating. We can refer to this as "always already listening," as coined by the Landmark Forum, or as mind reading, as Matthew McKay calls it in *Messages: The Communication Skills Book* (New Harbinger Publishers Inc., 2018). You assume you know what is going to be said and how the speaker feels (usually based on your own biases), and you begin rehearsing and formulating your response based on assumptions without fully hearing or validating the entirety of the message. You are anticipating what you will hear and how you plan to respond.

Most listening blocks are based on our biases. We have predispositions toward certain ideas and preconceptions about people, and we can't help but bring our own life experiences (both conscious and unconscious) and opinions into communication exchanges. Additionally, our personal communication style preferences are a factor. Everyone has listening blocks, and it is unlikely you will fully overcome all of them. What is important is that you learn to recognize your common blocks and deal with those that are impeding your ability to succeed at work or at home.

I find it reassuring when someone identifies with me in conversation, particularly if I am sharing something vulnerable. Because their insights are based on similar experience and they can empathize, this creates connection for me. As a result, I tend to over-identify in these kinds of conversations with others, assuming they also will find it comforting. In recognizing this bias as a block, I can work with it. Self-awareness is an important component in improving listening skills.

We can overcome the barriers to listening resulting from inner dialogue by practicing awareness, clearing our minds, and being fully present. Knowing yourself, understanding your triggers and emotional reactions, and taking ownership of your fears and insecurities will help you become a better listener.

MINIMIZING DISTRACTIONS AND INTERRUPTIONS

According to Gloria Mark, who studies digital distraction at the University of California, Irvine, it takes 1,395 seconds (23-plus minutes) to regain your focus following an interruption. To catch up, we work faster, but this doesn't necessarily improve productivity. Mark explains, "When people are constantly interrupted, they develop a mode of working faster (and writing less) to compensate for the time they know they will lose by being interrupted. Yet working faster with interruptions has its cost: people in the interrupted conditions experienced a higher workload, more stress, higher frustration, more time pressure, and effort."

Chatty people, office noise, and social media are among the top five causes of distraction and interruption at work, according to the World Economic Forum (WEF). Think about your typical workday. How much time do you spend deeply absorbed in projects that really matter? Are you able to give undivided attention to complex projects or problems? Are you continually distracted by office conversations, e-mail or instant message alerts, or social media? Each interruption forces you to regain your focus and productivity, not only costing you the time that the interruption itself takes, but also siphoning off the time you need to refocus. The WEF report revealed that reducing workplace distractions increased productivity, motivation, confidence, and overall happiness. Here are some tips to help you reduce workplace distractions:

1. Mute notifications and alerts on your phone or other devices.

2. Restrict checking personal social media feeds, chats, or text messages to scheduled breaks.

3. Be mindful of the volume and duration of the office conversations you take part in within the earshot of your coworkers. They also are trying to concentrate.

Best Practices for Better Listening

Minimize distractions. Mute your phone and step away from screens. Set aside time for the interaction, particularly if the stakes are high or the subject is complex or sensitive.

Reserve judgment. Hear the other person out and set aside your judgment or opinion until they are finished speaking—be aware of your own listening bias.

Ask clarifying questions. Paraphrase and repeat what you heard and ask questions to clarify areas where you aren't sure you clearly understood what someone said.

Demonstrate your engagement. Let the speaker know you are paying attention through nonverbal cues such as smiling, nodding, and leaning forward.

Validate understanding. Use the communication model from chapter 6—check out your perceptions (what you think you heard) to confirm your understanding of the communication's meaning and intent. A simple way to use the model is: "What I heard you say was . . . " followed by "Did you say . . . ?"

Self-manage. Develop awareness of your biases, predispositions, and triggers and learn to manage them in conversations.

Practice. Take opportunities to practice listening skills, especially with those where you notice there are blocks. Over time you will become a better listener.

CHAPTER 9

PUTTING RELATIONSHIP SKILLS TO THE TEST

Developing the skills that foster healthy relationships is an ongoing journey but one that is full of rewards. Learning to skillfully navigate conflict, give and receive feedback, and depersonalize criticism not only will make you a more effective communicator, but will serve to grow and deepen your personal and professional relationships. It may seem counterintuitive to welcome conflict and corrective feedback, but as you develop resilience in these areas, you will see that they form the bedrock of relationships of trust.

In this chapter, we'll discuss how cultivating these skills will help you improve interpersonal relationships, develop leadership muscle, and inspire others.

Navigating Conflict

"Conflict is only change trying to happen." How do you feel when you read that statement? When I first heard it, I felt a shift in perspective, reframing my view of conflict. Most people will try to avoid conflict at any cost. Certainly, dealing with conflict can be uncomfortable and sometimes unpleasant. Too often the measures we take to avoid conflict only serve to exacerbate the situation, allowing issues to fester and grow. By looking at conflict as a way that change is trying to occur, one strategy to dealing with it is to try to identify the kind of change that we need. We can view conflict as a flashing sign calling attention to the need for change rather than an uncomfortable or unpleasant situation to avoid. This is not to say that we need to actively seek out or incite conflict but rather that we recognize it for what it is—a signal that something is not working.

Given the diversity of most workplaces and the stress and pressure that many workers experience, we should expect conflict. Rarely is a workplace free of it. Workplace conflict can arise from unresolved issues such as perceived unfairness in workflow distribution, scheduling, or accountability practices. Personality clashes, differences in work habits, communications style, or leadership approaches, along with cultural and social differences, can all contribute to the potential for conflict. Even people who generally work well together can occasionally experience conflict. It is important to develop resilience and coping skills to recognize conflict and resolve it before it becomes unmanageable.

Here's an example: Emily and Michelle worked on an important project together. They developed a positive and friendly working relationship, and the project was a success. Management recognized both for their work, but Emily perceived that Michelle was receiving more credit for the project as she was advancing more rapidly in the company. Gradually, Emily began communicating less with Michelle, dropping their daily text check-ins, and excluding her from social group chats and lunch invitations. Their relationship deteriorated, with Emily showing signs of hostility in meetings—by ignoring Michelle, frowning and displaying negative body language when she spoke, or frequently disagreeing with her. At this stage, it is possible that Emily and Michelle can resolve the situation on their own by practicing self-awareness and taking ownership of the situation. However, if it escalates from here, it will create difficulties for their coworkers who are aware of the stress and tension and feel uncomfortable with it. We'll get back to this scenario, but for now, here are some signs that conflict may be brewing with a coworker:

- Daily communication becomes strained or difficult.
- You observe negative body language: crossed arms, frowning, eye-rolling, turning away, avoiding eye contact.
- Sarcasm or negative side commenting is employed in verbal exchanges.
- Complaints or disagreements increase between you.
- There is a feeling of resentment or of being resented.
- You witness a sudden or abrupt change in demeanor or communication style.
- You experience withdrawal from social contact or increased absence from work.

If you notice any of these signs in your communication with another or in their communication with you, it could be a signal that conflict is poised to erupt. Remember that conflict is only change trying to happen and it is pointing toward something that you need to address and resolve. Avoiding it will only lead to its escalation.

ADDRESSING THE CONFLICT

Unaddressed conflict festers, poisoning the work environment and spreading toxicity and anxiety. In the example in the previous section, if Michelle and Emily can't resolve their interpersonal conflict, it can become a problem for the rest of the team at work. One of the most important reasons to resolve workplace conflict head-on and in the early stages is to avoid its spread. If the conflict escalates and impacts the productivity, emotional well-being, or sense of trust on the team, it may require management or human resources to intervene. It's possible that both Emily and Michelle could end up with a formal report on their file related to the conflict.

A few signs to look for regarding escalating workplace conflict include the following:

- People become hostile or isolated.
- Lack of trust expressed in people or processes.
- Meetings become fractious or difficult.
- Workplace cliques or camps form.
- There is an increase in complaining and blaming.
- Absences or sick days increase.

In the early stages, individuals can usually resolve conflict by applying the skills referenced in the book: taking ownership, practicing awareness and active empathetic listening, checking assumptions, apologizing if needed, and conveying thoughts and opinions clearly and sensitively. In the next section, we will look at some additional techniques for resolving conflict. If conflict escalates or becomes threatening or toxic, it is important to secure additional support from a manager, human resources professional, or union representative.

RESOLVING THE CONFLICT

There is no question that resolving conflict requires courage and commitment. Practicing the skills in this book will help you become better at dealing with it. To be truly effective in any difficult communication, we must first learn to self-manage. It can be difficult to enter a confrontational situation if we are feeling triggered, anxious, tired, or angry. Almost universally, successful resolution requires us to be able to take the other person's perspective and honor their point of view. It's hard to do if we can't put our own emotional reactions aside. Effective resolutions also require us to take ownership of our part of the disagreement. Which of our attitudes, behaviors, or actions contributed to the conflict? This requires a high level of maturity and self-awareness.

Here is a handy tool that can help you reframe a conflictual situation. I call it "take each other's sides." While it is ideal for both parties to agree to do this and verbalize their observations, this is not always possible. The tool is still very effective even if you only use it yourself. Prior to confronting the issue, take a few moments to sit calmly and consider the other's viewpoint. Make some notes on how you think they see things. Curb your own "buts" and defensive thoughts and simply put yourself in their shoes and make a list. This process may not bring you into agreement with the other person, but it will promote understanding.

Here are some further tips for managing and resolving conflict:

Accept that conflict is normal. Some conflict is unavoidable in any ongoing relationship. See it as an opportunity for growth and change. By dealing with it you forge a pathway to improved communication and mutual understanding.

Take a calm approach. Emotion-laden responses don't help de-escalate a conflict. While it is important to honor your feelings and those of others, stay calm during your interaction and use neutral non-accusatory language as you explain your position. Enlist your powers of observation.

Practice active listening. Pay attention to what is said and be aware of both verbal and nonverbal cues. Withhold judgment and try to see the other's point of view. Ask questions for clarity and practice the communication model to validate interpretations.

Be objective. Analyze the conflict, separating the person from the problem. Discuss the specific problem, actions, or circumstances rather than focusing on the person. Consider what triggered the conflict and any underlying issues that you need to resolve.

Find common ground. It is always possible to find some common ground. It is helpful to think back to the origins of your relationship, and specify shared values, goals, or successes. Seek out points of agreement and connection. Think (and talk) about *why* it is important to resolve the conflict.

Focus on forward action. As you move toward resolution, it is important to focus on the future. How will things change because of this interaction? To what are you both willing to commit? If you are having a hard time finding a solution, check in with your own readiness to resolve. It can be easy to get embroiled in past wrongs. Are you truly willing to put the conflict behind you and move forward?

Be discreet. While it is perfectly acceptable to discuss interpersonal issues with trusted friends and advisors, do not use the conflict to encourage coworkers to take sides or to create camps in the workplace. Avoid spreading negativity and gossip. This is toxic behavior. A good rule of thumb is if you wouldn't say it to someone's face, you probably shouldn't be saying it at all. Unless others are directly involved, there is no reason to bring anyone else into the conflict or its resolution.

Giving and Receiving Criticism

Think about your role at work. Do you always feel completely clear about how well you are doing your job? Do you suspect that there may be areas where you could improve?

What about the work of others? Do you notice places where their contributions to the team or the way that they produce or present their work could be better? Can you easily identify their strengths and weaknesses? What about your own?

Typically, it is easier to see where others could improve than it is to see where we could. We tend to look at other people objectively, yet this is difficult to do for ourselves. As we discussed in chapter 5, we have blind spots, or scotomas, when it comes to self-awareness. *Scotoma* is a term that describes a blind spot within the eye, often caused by a physical defect. The late Lou Tice, founder of the Pacific Institute and author of *Personal Coaching for Results*, uses the term to describe anything that keeps us from perceiving or understanding the truth. He says that we "inadvertently create blind spots so we can hold onto our version of reality, our beliefs about ourselves and the world in which we live. Scotomas cause us to see what we expect to see, hear what we expect to hear, and experience what we expect to experience." Given this predisposition, it is difficult to objectively assess our own performance at work. Our scotomas act as a kind of filter, keeping us comfortably attached to our subjective reality. This interferes with our ability to grow and develop professionally. Basically, we don't know what we don't know.

Receiving and giving objective feedback is critical to improving performance and promoting learning on the job. We require feedback when there are issues of work performance, unresolved problems, reoccurring errors, or the need for clarifying expectations or goals. It is really the only way to assess the strengths and weaknesses that we can't see for ourselves, and it is an important tool for cultivating leadership skills. Depending on your role at work, you may be on the receiving or the delivering end of constructive criticism. Either way, it is useful to develop skills in this area if you want to be successful.

Good, constructive feedback aims to improve, correct, and support professional performance. It engages and involves the recipient in assessing, owning, and understanding the feedback and in proposing adjustments or solutions for change. Healthy feedback is descriptive rather than judgmental, focused on work and not personality. Criticism, on the other hand, can be personal and negatively evaluative, focused on faults or character rather than professional competence.

EFFECTIVE FEEDBACK IS SPECIFIC AND ACTIONABLE

Effective feedback is an essential part of the workplace, but to be effective, it must be specific, actionable, and balanced.

Specific Feedback

Specific feedback is selective and purposeful, concentrating on what is important and why it matters to performance. It is descriptive, focusing on observed behaviors, facts, or specific actions and not on personalities or character. Good feedback is timely and relevant to the current situation, delivered in a way that is sensitive to time and place and the emotional context. Presented objectively, specific feedback is not personal, and it does not belittle or otherwise disrespect the person receiving it.

Actionable Feedback

To be of use, effective feedback is actionable and solution oriented. The person receiving it should be able to take concrete steps or actions toward positive change. Be helpful and offer practical suggestions for improvement, but it's even more empowering if the recipient is involved in problem-solving and crafting a plan for change. It can be very useful to ask questions such as:

"What do you think?"

"What is your perspective?"

"What are your reactions to this?"

"Tell me, what are your thoughts or ideas?"

If you are the one receiving feedback, it is fair for you to ask questions like the ones listed, only rephrased such as: "May I offer my thoughts, reactions, perspective, ideas . . . ?" Once you agree on a plan, summarize the nature of the feedback and the agreed-upon forward action. Express support and identify any follow-up expected.

Balanced Feedback

Finally, good feedback is a balance of positive and negative. This doesn't mean that you need to offer both in any given interaction, but be wary of habitually offering *only* positive feedback or negative feedback. Your feedback will become distrusted, and people will begin to ignore it.

A Note about Praise

Most of us enjoy praise and positive acknowledgment of our contributions. When it comes to the workplace, though, there is evidence suggesting that most people prefer corrective feedback immediately, as long as it is delivered respectfully, clearly, and professionally. A *Harvard Business Review* study affirmed that "people want corrective feedback, even more than praise, if it's provided in a constructive manner. By roughly a three to one margin, they believe it does even more to improve their performance than positive feedback."

This doesn't mean you shouldn't offer congratulations, genuine acknowledgment, credit, and thanks for a job well done to colleagues. Positive reinforcement is a powerful tool. However, you should not use it to soft-pedal or sugarcoat honest corrective feedback. Remember: Honesty builds trust.

Ideally, if both parties understand feedback well, you should be able to move into a solution-oriented framework rather quickly. It is important, however, if emotions are at play, to have a cooling-off period if needed. Also, be aware of feedback overload. Stick to two or three important points at a time; otherwise feedback can become confusing and hard to absorb.

Giving and receiving feedback provide an excellent opportunity for you to practice the communication skills covered in this book. Be self-aware. Read and pay attention to verbal and nonverbal cues. Manage your message. Use the communication model to clarify and validate assumptions and practice active listening to ensure mutual understanding.

IT'S NOT PERSONAL

Good, constructive feedback is not personal, and it's important not to take it that way. Management is evaluating your performance and not your character, personality, work ethic, or values. It is nearly impossible to grow professionally without benchmarks for progress or some form of evaluation and assessment. Many workplaces have formal processes and regularly scheduled reviews that provide an opportunity for good, constructive, professional feedback. However, this is not true of all places. There will be times in between scheduled annual reviews when management will need to offer corrective or constructive feedback. We can characterize this as information that redirects behavior, explores or examines improved ways of doing things, or identifies gaps in optimal performance or process. Its goal is not to criticize but to encourage positive improvement.

There is a subtle nuance between criticizing people or criticizing their work. Let's take Devin's newsletter from chapter 3 as an example. Devin's boss needed to give him some corrective feedback. Compare the way the focus changes in this example:

From: "You made many mistakes in the last newsletter."

To: "There were many mistakes in the last newsletter."

The difference is subtle, but by eliminating the *you* in the second example, the criticism is depersonalized. The focus is on the newsletter, not on Devin.

HOW NOT TO GET PERSONAL WHEN GIVING FEEDBACK

Get to the point. Be direct and focus objectively on the problem that needs solving. Describe it clearly and be specific. Avoid generalizations like *always* or *never*.

Watch your language. Avoid using the pronoun *you* when framing the feedback. Do not discuss personality traits or make blanket statements about the "type" of person they are. Do not belittle, name-call, or use sarcasm, even in jest. Be respectful. People make mistakes, and it doesn't define who they are.

Focus on the desired outcome. Restate the goal or object of the assignment or project. Clarify what is at stake. Focus on the change desired or the corrected behavior that you want. Emphasize the potential beneficial impact of solving the problem or adjusting style, behavior, or approach.

Develop a plan. Set a timeline and clear expectations for moving forward. Agree on next steps and a plan for checking and measuring progress.

Bonus Tip: It can be useful to use digital tools such as internal online surveys or polls and have people anonymously self-assess or provide feedback on a process or project. You can then compare the individual feedback and talk about the gaps in perception or opinion. This can be a way of depersonalizing the information and is particularly effective for teams.

Sometimes corrective feedback can be difficult to accept. If you are the one giving feedback and you have done your best to depersonalize it and be constructive, you need to allow the receiver space to absorb and process the information. It is entirely possible that he or she will have an emotional response. This is normal. Avoid saying, "Don't take it personally." This is insensitive.

If you are the one receiving feedback, remember that how you respond is completely up to you. You can respond defensively, or you can choose not to take the feedback personally and see it as a tool for growth and an affirmation that you are valued. Your workplace is investing time and energy in identifying ways for you to improve. Allow yourself the opportunity to benefit from this investment.

THE ART OF UNPLUGGING

Just for fun, spend a week monitoring your screen time. How much of that time do you spend doing deep work, focusing on the essential projects or people in your work or life? While writing this book, I checked my smartphone screen time total and found it at over an hour a day! This was a startling number that jolted me into paying much closer attention to what I was doing online.

The Internet is rife with exhortations to hustle, boss, crush, and slay. Online gurus preach the virtues of the 24/7 lifestyle and the ubiquitous use of smartphones, PCs, tablets, and other devices that provide us with unlimited access to each other unbounded by time or geography. Global workplaces conduct business across time zones, and there are high expectations from customers, clients, and coworkers for immediate responses. We've become an always-on culture, with most of us never really going offline.

We don't yet fully understand the emotional, physical, and psychological effects of a continually online presence, but we know that we are human and as such need rest, recreation, personal connection, and time in our lives to pause and reflect.

Work-life balance is an elusive concept—it implies that we can somehow carve our lives into neat compartments achieving a kind of utopian stasis. It is better to seek a well-rounded life, ensuring that there is time and space in your life for what matters when it matters. Being conscious of your needs and the needs of others and setting clear boundaries will help you create such space.

Here are some tips to help us all "unplug" more often:

Set boundaries. Think about your work style and rhythms as well as your family and social obligations. Set up your online time to be optimal for productivity as well as to accommodate your personal needs. You do not need to be online "just in case." It is an unrealistic expectation and does not contribute to a balanced life. Set your boundaries and communicate them clearly and then manage your time and notifications. Mute alerts when you are not available and set up autoresponders to let others know that you are offline. Then be fully present in your offline activities whether for work or play.

Respect boundaries. It may work for you to send e-mails or instant messages early in the morning or late at night, but it may not work for your colleagues. If they have set boundaries to divide their personal and work time, respect them. If you are not sure what they are, ask. Remember that not everyone turns off their pings and notifications, particularly if they have young children or family away from home. If your working style or time zone demands that you work in others' off hours, then use technology to schedule communication at agreed-upon times or set reminders for yourself as to your coworkers' available time.

Lead the way. There is no reason why you can't lead a conversation at work about how to set boundaries for time and device use. You have the right to ask for what you need and to explore options that contribute to a healthy workplace for all.

Communicating as a Leader

Scholars credit American lawyer James C. Humes, who wrote speeches for five U.S. presidents, with saying, "The art of communication is the language of leadership." Much of your corporate culture will depend on the tone and style that the leadership sets.

In the early 2000s I had the opportunity to work with a large, diverse school district's leadership. The school board had appointed a new superintendent, and the organization was poised for change. Budgets were tight, schools needed to close, and several key leadership positions were vacant due to a retirement wave. At the time, the district's communication culture could be described as what I call "Guess My Secret." Senior staff and leadership closely guarded information. Decision-making processes lacked transparency, and school budget allocations and promotions were largely based on partisanship and preferential treatment rather than need or merit. Outside of meeting curriculum targets, those who worked there could only guess at expectations and speculate about what made for success.

The new superintendent implemented a district-wide consultation process to set new directions that included online surveys, facilitated focus group sessions, and feedback reviews. He included representatives from all levels of the organization in the consultations. The process took nearly two years to implement, and as with any kind of change, resistance was a dynamic—particularly from those who had benefited most under the previous culture.

The single most important factor in the strategy's success was the attitude and example that the superintendent himself set. He attended as many consultation meetings as possible, listening carefully and offering supportive and clear reinforcement of the direction the district was taking. He addressed the concerns of parents, staff, and teachers empathetically. He modeled effective communication skills whether at the podium or in a one-to-one meeting. As a baby boomer, he was not fully comfortable using digital tools personally, but he supported the district's initiatives in using online surveys, polling, e-mail, and the other digital tools available at the time to reach stakeholder audiences across the district. He championed not only the change, he championed *communicating* the change.

If you are in a leadership position, the way you communicate creates a profound impact on your organization. By practicing effective communication skills, you can set the bar for your workplace. Your example will create a ripple effect that will impact the positive performance, satisfaction, and happy productivity of individual employees and teams.

EFFECTIVE COMMUNICATION IN GROUPS

It may come as no surprise to you at this point in the book that what we are talking about is not only good communication, but how it contributes to developing workplace leadership skills. Consider this quote by leadership expert John C. Maxwell: "Leadership is not about titles, positions, or flowcharts. It is about one life influencing another."

Maxwell is pointing to the notion of personal, rather than positional, leadership. Most of us are familiar with positional leadership as an attribute that accompanies a specific role.

Management promotes you to department head or adds you to the management team. You receive a title, and your coworkers consider you a leader. Management hopes that you will bring strong leadership qualities to the role—great interpersonal skills, an advanced understanding of strategy and goal setting, the ability to see the big picture and inspire others. However, you can nurture, develop, and express most if not all of these qualities whether or not you hold an official title. You are free to cultivate personal leadership.

Think about your role as part of a team at work, whether formally or informally. A good leader is primarily a good listener. Your ability to encourage others to express their views, share ideas, and contribute to solutions helps create a safe environment where people feel included and valued. This kind of approach fosters creativity and innovation. It promotes productivity and leads to a positive corporate culture. It is natural in a group setting for individuals to want to express their ideas and views and make personal contributions. Leaders hear what people are saying, reflect it back, and synthesize the information. Acting as facilitators, they integrate and incorporate multiple viewpoints into an overall message, finding common ground and validating points of view. This communication skill is a powerful one to develop and will serve you well in group settings, especially if you hope to grow in your personal leadership skills.

Coming to understand the difference between personal and positional leadership can be life-changing. In the case of positional leadership, you wield power based on your position in the organization. These roles are attached to specific hierarchical levels within a company, and promotions to them are largely controlled by others. Many organizations are flat—there is no ladder to climb. Others are small, with very few leadership positions unless those occupying them retire or leave. In these situations, leadership opportunities are limited.

Personal leadership, however, is intrinsic. It is based on your skills and ability to influence people and events, whether you have any formal authority or not. It is always with you. If you focus on developing personal leadership, you empower yourself to motivate, inspire, and influence others in many situations. By practicing effective communication, you can help shape your workplace's culture and serve as an example to coworkers.

LEAD THE WAY WITH EFFECTIVE COMMUNICATION

Think about yourself 15 years into the future. Where do you see yourself in your career? Throughout this book I've offered several examples, based on actual clients, of people who have learned the value of effective communication in the workplace. In each case, with openness to feedback and a commitment to personal and professional development, the people in these examples were able to advance their careers and improve their relationships with coworkers, colleagues, and bosses.

Nala learned to read the room and adapt her presenting style to build positive relationships and support for her ideas. Devin realized that he needed to overcome his ego and collaborate with others. Javeed discovered the value of self-awareness in surmounting his anger issues and found common ground with his team and his boss. Michelle set an example for coworkers and caught the leadership's attention by practicing excellent listening skills and networking proactively. Many of my clients have come to understand the digital divide between the generations and learned to communicate well in spite of it.

Like all of us, they are living and working at the intersection of the digital and analog worlds. We are all learning to cope with a plethora of communications channels, new technologies, and digital distractions. Our workplaces are diverse, posing unique challenges as we navigate cultural and language barriers, generation gaps, unevenly distributed technology and tools, and the demands and frustrations of a fast-paced and ever-changing world.

We are in this together, and the challenges we encounter in the contemporary workplace are the challenges we face in the world at large as we co-create the future. You have a great deal to contribute by learning to use effective communication tools. Whether or not you hold a position of authority, you can lead the way in today's workplace and set a positive example for others to follow. Here are three essential guideposts to consider:

Empathy, not ego. Whenever possible, set your ego aside and try to see the other's perspective. Whether you are de-escalating a conflict, collaborating on ideas, or crafting a presentation, put yourself in the other's shoes. Approach others with respect, humility, and vulnerability.

Check your assumptions. It is easy to assume that we understand others or that they see us clearly. Practice active listening, be curious, ask questions, and use the communication model from chapter 6 to validate interpretations. Base your responses and actions on facts, not conjecture. Remember that we all have biases and unique cultural, generational, and social lenses.

Set an example. Realize that your decision to model open communication, practice awareness, and hone your written, oral, and digital skills will influence the people around you and help bring success to your organization.

CHOOSING THE CHANNEL: DIGITAL VERSUS IN PERSON

Think about a situation in which you were unclear whether it was better to speak to the person face-to-face or via a digital channel. What helped you decide? It is not uncommon for people to choose a digital channel over an in-person channel simply out of fear. If the conversation is high stakes or there's a misunderstanding or a potential conflict, it is a (very human) tendency to avoid facing these situations by choosing the least direct channel. Unfortunately, in these situations, this is not usually a good choice.

As we've discussed throughout the book, the binary nature of most digital communication and its absence of tone make it very difficult to digitally communicate the nuances, empathy, and awareness required for sensitive communication. Choosing a digital channel for a difficult communication may help you avoid the feelings of discomfort that face-to-face confrontation may bring, but it will not help you develop important relationship and communication skills for the future.

Here are a few questions you can ask yourself as you consider how to choose the best channel for your communication:

- Is this communication informational, instructional, persuasive, or transactional? Does it require a give-and-take to be successful?
- Is this a high-stakes communication?
- Is there a potential for conflict to be escalated or de-escalated because of this communication?

- How important is hearing the other's point of view in this matter?

- Do I need to feel heard or to offer more detailed explanation or information?

- Is the information I want to convey complex or difficult to understand? Would it benefit from co-present interaction?

- Are there emotional impact considerations? Is privacy required?

- What about the long-term relationship? Is it valuable? How does the communication help or hinder?

- Is there a digital tool that could be helpful in resolving or supporting this communication (e.g., feedback survey, poll)?

- What is the organizational standard regarding this kind of communication?

- Who is the audience for or receiver of this message? What way will best reach them?

Face-to-face communication is the best choice when it comes to resolving interpersonal conflict, giving feedback, or discussing sensitive topics. If actual physical proximity is not possible, then the next best choices are videoconferencing and telephone conversations, where the interaction can go back and forth. In conversations where awareness and empathy are important, choose the best available co-present options.

You can use a mix of digital and in-person tools, especially to break an impasse or to coordinate schedules. Let's go back to the conflict that was brewing between Emily and Michelle earlier in this chapter. Michelle decided to break their impasse via a casual text message asking Emily about a routine matter. Emily's reply was blunt, but she did reply. Encouraged, Michelle followed up with a further text e-mail inviting Emily to get together to discuss future applications of their project. Emily agreed, so Michelle sent a polite e-mail suggesting that they compare available dates and set up a meeting. They used digital tools to lead the way and handle logistics and moved the important discussion to an in-person format. Michelle took the time to think through how she could approach Emily and the best tools to do so.

There is an art to communicating well. It is not an exact science. It takes time, focus, and practice. However, if you are willing to apply the skills you've discovered here and expand your level of self-awareness and empathy, you will come to consistently choose communications channels wisely and well.

SELF-
ASSESSMENT TOOLS

This is your opportunity to pause and reflect on what you have learned in this book. Hopefully you have gained greater insight into the power of effective communication at work and the benefits and challenges of the vast array of digital communication tools available today and how they are changing the way we communicate.

The following questions are designed to be self-reflective and to increase your awareness of your personal communication strengths and challenges. There are no right or wrong answers. Use the insights you discover to map out a personal plan to become a more effective communicator at work.

What Is Your Communication Style at Work?

What do you see as your communication strengths? Think about written skills, oral skills, reading skills, and listening skills.

_____

_____

_____

_____

Do you feel confident communicating via digital channels such as e-mail, texting, and instant messaging? What about videoconferencing or chat room threads?

_____

_____

_____

_____

Are you comfortable in face-to-face situations, or do you find yourself avoiding in-person interactions?

_____

_____

_____

_____

Do you feel that you understand the expected etiquettes for different forms of workplace communication? Why or why not?

_____

_____

_____

_____

Are there cultural or social norms that you feel you need to overcome or integrate to be more effective in communicating at work?

_____

_____

_____

_____

Do you see yourself as empathetic? Can you think of an example?

_____

_____

_____

_____

Are you aware of, and able to identify the communication style of others? Do you adapt as needed?

_____

_____

_____

_____

What is your preferred way to communicate? What do you avoid?

_____

_____

_____

_____

Do you consider yourself an introvert, extrovert, or ambivert? How do you typically manage conflict?

_____

_____

_____

_____

Are you comfortable expressing your ideas and opinions at work? Are you open to the ideas and opinions of others?

_____

_____

_____

_____

What is your comfort level giving or receiving feedback? How do you handle conflict?

_____

_____

_____

_____

List three areas of communication at work that you find challenging:

1. _____

2. _____

3. _____

List three areas of communication at work where you are completely confident:

1. _____

2. _____

3. _____

What Is Your Company's Communication Culture?

Would you characterize your workplace as formal or informal in terms of corporate communication style?

_____

_____

_____

_____

If you could fix one aspect of communication at work, what would it be?

_____

_____

_____

_____

Is the company culture inclusive? Are people encouraged to share ideas and collaborate?

_____

_____

_____

_____

How transparent is decision-making?

_____

_____

_____

_____

Does your workplace have guidelines or protocols that govern communications? Are there rules, and are they enforced? Are the company etiquettes around the use of e-mail, IM, or texting clear and transparent?

_____

_____

_____

_____

How diverse is your workplace? Are you expected to communicate with people across time zones in languages other than your own? How are cultural or social differences respected in your workplace?

_____

_____

_____

_____

How many generations can you identify in the workplace? How does this impact communication at work?

_____

_____

_____

_____

Does the organization evenly distribute digital tools throughout the organization? In other words, does everyone have access to the same platforms? Does management provide training as needed?

_____

_____

_____

_____

Are workplace conflicts handled effectively, or are they left to fester? Are boundaries respected or ignored?

_____

_____

_____

How Do They Match Up?

Compare your style with what you've identified as the company's communication style. How do they match up? Where do you share common ground with the company's style? What are the gaps? If you are still not sure about the commonalities and gaps, look at the company's social media feeds, website, or other promotional material. What is the tone? Scrutinize your own social media or other communication. Compare tone. What do you notice?

_____

_____

_____

_____

_____

_____

_____

_____

List three areas for improvement that you can make to align more effectively with your workplace communication culture:

1. _____

2. _____

3. _____

Modern Digital Communication Tools List

There are many devices, tools, and platforms in use in today's workplaces. What follows is a list of some of those in common use for digital communication. Every workplace is different. Yours may use some of these or others that have similar features or applications but are customized for your sector. Software engineers are developing and launching new communication, collaboration, and project management platforms and apps every day. We also are on the brink of the widespread integration of Internet of Things (IoT) technology into daily life based on advances in machine learning and artificial intelligence.

All of us must become adept at learning the skills required to adjust to the ever-changing norms, etiquettes, and expectations of digital communication in the workplace. For many years I have advised clients that the most empowering skills they can develop in the digital age are attitudes—open-mindedness, adaptability, patience, and the willingness to learn. If you cultivate these attitudes, you will find success. Good luck!

COMPUTERS AND DEVICES

This is a list of some of the digital or technical devices you will typically encounter in your daily work:

- Personal computers (desktop and/or laptop)
- Tablets
- Smartphones
- Desk phone
- Digital display boards or monitors
- Remote cameras, microphones, or portable lighting

VIDEOCONFERENCING

Some of the more common videoconferencing platforms include:

- Zoom
- Google Hangouts
- UberConference
- TrueConf Online

- Skype
- FreeConference
- Appear.in
- Slack video calls

PROJECT MANAGEMENT AND COLLABORATION TOOLS

There are many project management and collaboration tools with a variety of features. Here are some of the more popular ones:

- Slack
- Basecamp
- Asana
- Trello
- Google Drive

- Jira
- Facebook Workplace
- Smartsheets
- Zoho Workplace

WORKPLACE CHAT APPS

- WhatsApp
- Front
- Slack
- Microsoft Teams

- Flock
- Discord
- Twist
- Google Hangouts

RESOURCES

The following is a list of references to the places, people, and publications that have informed the principles in this book. I highly recommend them as resources to you as you navigate the world of effective communication in the digital age.

INSTITUTES

CRR Global: crrglobal.com

The Haven: haven.ca

Institute for Health and Human Potential: ihhp.com

The Pacific Institute: thepacificinstitute.com

Process Work Institute: processwork.edu

WEBSITES AND ONLINE RESOURCES

Digital strategist, author, thought leader, Chris Brogan: chrisbrogan.com

Effective Communications at Work Facebook Group, hosted by Vicki McLeod: facebook.com/groups/effectivecommunicationatwork (please feel free to join)

Coaching, training, and other works by the author: vickimcleod.com

Technology expert, founder of *Grey Matters*, Steve Dotto: dottotech.com

BOOKS

Coaching for Performance, GROWing People, Performance, and Purpose by Sir John Whitmore (Nicholas Brealey Publishing, 3rd edition, 2007)

Daring Greatly: How the Courage to Be Vulnerable Transforms the Way We Live, Love, Parent, and Lead by Brene Brown (Avery, 2015)

Digital Legacy Plan: A Guide to the Personal and Practical Elements of Your Digital Life Before You Die by Angela Crocker and Vicki McLeod (Self-Counsel Press, 2019)

The Digital Renaissance of Work: Delivering Digital Workplaces Fit for the Future by Paul Miller (Gower Publishing, 2014)

Disrupting Digital Business by Ray Wang (Harvard Business Review Press, 2015)

Emotional Intelligence—Why It Can Matter More Than IQ by Daniel Goleman (Bantam, 1995)

The History of Writing by Steven Roger Fischer (Reaktion Books, 2001/2011)

Personal Coaching for Results by Lou Tice (Thomas Nelson, 1997)

The Silent Language of Leaders: How Body Language Can Help—or Hurt—How You Lead by Carol Kinsey Goman (Jossey-Bass, 2011)

A Theory of Human Motivation by Abraham H. Maslow, 1943 (Martino Publishing, 2013)

UNTRENDING, A Field Guide to Social Media That Matters. How to Post, Tweet, and Like Your Way to a More Meaningful Life by Vicki McLeod (First Choice, 2016)

We Are All the Same Age Now: Valuegraphics, The End of Demographic Stereotypes by David Allison (Lioncrest Publishing, 2018)

On Writing Well, The Classic Guide to Writing Non-Fiction by William Zinsser (Harper Perennial, 7th edition, 2016)

You and the Internet of Things: A Practical Guide to Understanding and Integrating the IoT into Your Daily Life by Vicki McLeod (Self-Counsel Press, 2020)

REFERENCES

CHAPTER 1

Allison, David. *We Are All the Same Age Now: Valuegraphics, The End of Demographic Stereotypes.* Austin, TX: Lioncrest Publishing, 2018.

McLeod, Vicki, and Angela Crocker. *Digital Legacy Plan, A Guide to the Personal and Practical Elements of Your Digital Life Before You Die.* North Vancouver, BC, Canada: Self-Counsel Press, 2019.

Mirabile, Keith, Rocco Raffo, and Charmaine Thomas. "What Workers Want." Aerotek.com. Accessed December 2019. aerotek.com/en/insights/what-workers-want-and-what-does -not-matter.

Quinn, Sarah. "How to Market to Goldfish: What Decreasing Attention Spans Mean for Marketers." Last modified August 27, 2017. blog.hubspot.com/marketing/human-attention -span-decreased.

Skills You Need, Helping You Develop Life Skills. Employability Skills, "What Are Soft Skills?" Accessed December 2019. skillsyouneed.com/general/soft-skills.html.

Solomon, Lou. "Two-Thirds of Managers Are Uncomfortable Communicating with Employees." *Harvard Business Review.* Accessed December 2019. hbr.org/2016/03/two-thirds-of -managers-are-uncomfortable-communicating-with-employees.

The Economist. Special Report. "Peering around the Corner." Accessed December 2019. economist.com/special-report /2001/10/13/peering-round-the-corner.

CHAPTER 2

Aristotle. *Rhetoric*. Book III. Translated by W. Rhys Roberts. The Internet Classics Archive. Accessed December 2019. classics.mit.edu/Aristotle/rhetoric.3.iii.html.

Burke, Kenneth. "107 Texting Statistics That Answer All Your Questions." Text Request. Last modified January 2019. textrequest.com/blog/texting-statistics-answer-questions.

Kinsey Goman, Carol. "Has Technology Killed Face-to-Face Communication?" *Forbes*. November 14, 2018. forbes.com/sites /carolkinseygoman/2018/11/14/has-technology-killed-face -to-face-communication/#286b67eda8cc.

Vermont Official State Website. Vermont State Highway Safety Office, Behavioural Safety Unit. "Worldwide Texting Statistics." Accessed December 2019. ghsp.vermont.gov/sites/ghsp/files /documents/Worldwide%20Texting%20Statistics.pdf.

CHAPTER 3

Brogan, Chris. "Communication—It's Already Changed." E-mail newsletter. April 23, 2017.

Fischer, Steven Roger. *The History of Writing*. London: Reaktion Books, 2011.

Privacy Rights Clearinghouse (PRC). "Is Your Employer Monitoring You through Your iPhone?" Accessed January 2020. privacyrights.org/resources/your-employer-monitoring -you-through-your-iphone.

Wang, Ray. *Disrupting Digital Business*. Brighton, MA: Harvard Business Review Press, 2015.

CHAPTER 5

American Management Association. "New Study Shows Nice Guys Finish First," Amanet. Accessed January 2020. amanet.org /articles/new-study-shows-nice-guys-finish-first.

Flaum, J. P. "When It Comes to Business Leadership, Nice Guys Finish First." Green Peak Partners, Organizational Consulting. Accessed January 2020. greenpeakpartners.com/wp-content /uploads/2018/09/Green-Peak_Cornell-University-Study _What-predicts-success.pdf.

Miller, Paul. *The Digital Renaissance of Work: Delivering Digital Workplaces Fit for the Future*. Aldershot, UK: Gower Publishing, 2014.

Whitmore, Sir John. *Coaching for Performance, The Principles and Practice of Coaching and Leadership* (5th ed.). London: Nicholas Brealey Publishing, 2017.

CHAPTER 6

Hunt, Vivian, Dennis Layton, and Sara Prince. "Diversity Matters." McKinsey & Company. February 2015. mckinsey.com/~/media /mckinsey/business%20functions/organization/our%20insights /why%20diversity%20matters/diversity%20matters.ashx.

Wilson III, Ernest J. "Empathy Is Still Lacking in Leaders Who Need It Most." *Harvard Business Review*. September 2015. hbr.org/2015/09/empathy-is-still-lacking-in-the-leaders -who-need-it-most.

Wong, Bennett, and Jock McKeen. *Being: A Manual for Life* (3rd ed.). Gabriola, BC, Canada: Haven Institute Press, 2013.

Zalisky, Katharine. "Investing in Diversity: How to Make the Case to Your Boss." Glassdoor. Accessed January 2020. glassdoor.com /blog/investing-in-diversity.

CHAPTER 7

Benjamin, Bill. "Vulnerability: Nah, Let's Go with Humility." Institute for Health and Human Potential. June 3, 2014. ihhp.com/blog/2014/06/03/go_with_humility.

Brown, Brene. *Daring Greatly: How the Courage to Be Vulnerable Transforms the Way We Live, Love, Parent, and Lead.* Reprint Edition. New York: Avery Publishing, 2015.

Brown, Brene. "The Power of Vulnerability." Video. Filmed at TEDxHouston June 2010. ted.com/talks/brene_brown_the _power_of_vulnerability?language=en.

Goleman, Daniel. *Emotional Intelligence—Why It Can Matter More Than IQ.* New York: Bantam, 1995.

Jostle Corporation. *Bridging the Engagement Gap: How Leaders Can Get the Levels of Engagement They Strive For.* Jostle E-Book. Accessed January 2020. intranet.jostle.me/bridging-the -engagement-gap.

Mao, Jianghua, et al. "Growing Followers: Exploring the Effects of Leader Humility on Follower Self-Expansion, Self-Efficacy, and Performance." *Journal of Management Studies.* Wiley Online Library. Accessed January 2020. onlinelibrary.wiley.com/doi /abs/10.1111/joms.12395.

Maslow, Abraham H. *A Theory of Human Motivation.* Chicago, IL: Martino Publishing, 1943.

Solis, Brian, and Deb Lavoy. "The Engagement Gap: Executives and Employees Think Differently about Employee Engagement." Jostle Corporation White Paper. Accessed January 2020. jostle.me/engagement-gap.

CHAPTER 8

Feldman, Sarah. "This Is What People Find Distracting at Work." World Economic Forum. Accessed February 2020. https://www.weforum.org/agenda/2019/03/what-people-find-distracting-at-work

Mark, Gloria, Daniela Gudith, and Ulrich Klocke. "The Cost of Interrupted Work: More Speed and Stress." University of California, Irvine. Proceedings of ACM CHI 2008. Accessed February 2020. https://www.ics.uci.edu/~gmark/chi08-mark.pdf

McKay, Matthew, Martha Davis, and Patrick Fanning. *Messages, The Communication Skills Book* (4th ed.). Oakland, CA: New Harbinger Publishers Inc., 2018.

CHAPTER 9

Tice, Lou. *Personal Coaching for Results*. Nashville, TN: Thomas Nelson, 1997.

Zenger, Jack, and Joseph Folkman. "Your Employees Want the Negative Feedback You Hate to Give." *Harvard Business Review*. January 15, 2014. hbr.org/2014/01/your-employees-want-the-negative-feedback-you-hate-to-give.

INDEX

Acknowledgments

My special personal thanks go to Fred Armstrong, Steve Dotto, Nathan Hyam, Joseph Kakwinokanasum, Faye Luxembourg-Hyam, Beda Martin, Sean Moffitt, Etanda Morelli, Victoria Pawlowski, and Sylvia Taylor, who each in their own way heartened and uplifted me during the crafting of this book.

Deepest thanks to the publisher, Callisto Media, for trusting me with this book and particularly to Anne Lowrey, my managing editor there, whose fine hand guided these words with warmth and sureness. It has been a joy! Thank you to Thomas Sigel, my developmental editor, who made the book better. Thank you to Callisto's acquisitions editor, Joe Cho, who knew that this was my book to write. To the rest of the team at Callisto, your expertise behind the scenes does not go unnoticed. Thank you.

I would also like to thank the many clients whose trust and confidence have inspired me personally and professionally during the past three decades. It's been an honor to learn, grow, and work with you. Such work would have been impossible without the people who have supported us at Main Street Communications Ltd. over the years: Lori Graham, Cindy Farnsworth, Rebecca Vaughn, Kimmy Finnsson, Lorene Stuart, Kathleen Irwin, and Barb Wright.

I am blessed beyond measure to have a wide circle of friends, family, and colleagues, writers and non-writers alike, who support my work and life. Your friendship and love are a crucible for personal growth and proof of the principles in this book: Valerie, Tyce, Tanner, Suzanne, Stuart, Steve, Sherree, Shelley, Shannon, Seija, Sean, Russ, Rebecca, Randy, Peter, Paul, Michael, Marty, Marian, the Martin clan, the McLeod clan, Kim Louise, Keith, Heather, Donna, Dom, Debra, Darlene, Conny, Chris, Christina, Cass, Carol, Cadi, Bosco, Angela, Ann, and Alex. Much gratitude goes to Joan Noel, my coach and a champion of authentic human connection, and to the team at CRR Global, whose groundbreaking work is changing the world. I have no words to adequately express my appreciation to the late Drucilla Desabrais for the gifts of her love and mentorship. Her light shines on.

This book was written on the unceded territory of the Snuneymuxw First Nation, a Coast Salish people. Their beautiful land is in the center of Coast Salish territory on the eastern coast of Vancouver Island in British Columbia, Canada. I thank them for the privilege of living and working here.

About the Author

Vicki McLeod is a writer, coach, consultant, and award-winning entrepreneur. She is the author of *You and the Internet of Things: A Practical Guide to Understanding and Integrating the IoT into Your Daily Life* (Self-Counsel Press, 2020); *Digital Legacy Plan: A Guide to the Personal and Practical Elements of Your Digital Life Before You Die* (Self-Counsel Press, 2019), co-authored with Angela Crocker; and *#Untrending: A Field Guide to Social Media That Matters, How to Post, Tweet, and Like Your Way to a Meaningful Life* (First Choice Books, 2016). She writes a newspaper column on digital lifestyle and blogs at vickimcleod.com.

For nearly three decades, McLeod has helped organizations, governments, and small businesses create conversations that matter with clients, customers, and stakeholders. She coaches and mentors leaders, executive teams, and individuals to take inspiration and turn it into strategy.

McLeod is an advocate for mindful business, everyday happiness, and living a life rich with meaning. She leads retreats and workshops, writes prose and poetry, and makes books, art, and bread. You can find her online on Facebook, Twitter, LinkedIn, and Instagram and offline on beautiful Vancouver Island on the west coast of Canada, making something.

CPSIA information can be obtained
at www.ICGtesting.com
Printed in the USA
JSHW030801050620
6063JS00005B/77

9 781646 115914